HAUNTED FLINT

HAUNTED FLINT

ROXANNE RHOADS AND JOE SCHIPANI

HAUNTED
AMERICA

Published by Haunted America
A Division of The History Press
Charleston, SC
www.historypress.com

Front cover: Ari Napolitano.
Back cover: Daniel Conner's collection; *inset*: Daniel Conner's collection.

First published 2019

Manufactured in the United States

ISBN 9781467143042

Library of Congress Control Number: 2019943351

Notice: The information in this book is true and complete to the best of our knowledge. It is offered without guarantee on the part of the authors or The History Press. The authors and The History Press disclaim all liability in connection with the use of this book.

To my husband, Robert, and my children, Robby, Ari and Tim, thank you for all your love and support and for dealing with my obsession of all things spooky. And thank you for understanding all the events I couldn't attend while locked away in my writing cave.
To Ilona, thank you for being my best friend and personal cheerleader; for always being there to listen to me vent and for cheering me on when things would get tough.
—Roxanne

To my partner, Phillip, who has always supported me and put up with my craziness by listening to me tell stories about hauntings and murders. Thank you for all you have done and for encouraging me to follow my passions and dreams.
—Joe

CONTENTS

CONTENTS

PREFACE

Tales of ghosts and eerie encounters have been part of my life for as long as I can remember.

My mother had a tendency to attribute strange occurrences to spirits trying to communicate with us. One of my earliest memories is being up late with my mother one summer night and our alarms going off for no apparent reason.

My father had passed away the December before, so it was just us girls in the house. That was spooky in itself; add weird noises that had no known origin, and I was terrified. It was the early 1980s; our smoke detectors and the security system were not connected in any way like today, when everything is connected through Wi-Fi. Nothing was glitching that could have affected both alarms. The smoke detectors were just round things that hung on the wall operated by batteries, independent of any other system.

There was no smoke, no fire and no one trying to break into our house.

But on that hot summer night, the security alarm and the smoke detectors kept going off. First one, then the other, then they sometimes went off at the same time. Random beeps, blurps and screeches filled the night. My mom swore it was my dad trying to communicate with us. What was he trying to say? I have no idea. The noises made no sense to four-year-old me. When I got older, I often wondered if those beeps and screeches would have translated into Morse code. Long bursts, short beeps, long haunting siren wails.

Whatever the cause of the sounds that night, my fate was sealed—my appetite for all things spooky had been piqued. Since then, I have always gravitated toward the paranormal. I adore supernatural-themed books, movies and television shows. If it features ghosts, vampires, witches, werewolves or unsolved mysteries with a paranormal twist, I'm there.

I've collected ghost stories and tales of Michigan's haunted locations for years. But I never thought about putting them together in a book. It was just a hobby. Then my friend Davonna and I were discussing setting up a walking tour of Flint's haunted locations. That turned into a book idea, which led me to searching for more haunted stories about Flint.

My call for Flint ghost stories was noticed by Joe Schipani, who had also been collecting stories about Flint's history, haunted locations and weird deaths. We decided to partner up, pooling our info and expanding it into one book. Joe is the master researcher. He visited locations, participated in ghost hunts, talked to people throughout Flint and spent countless hours in the library searching for unsolved mysteries, weird stories and whispers of hauntings. I scoured the Internet for Flint ghost stories, hunted through archives of historical documents, interviewed locals through social media, visited locations and put everything we discovered into writing. Together, we found more haunted locations and spooky stories about Flint than we ever imagined we would. The result is this book in your hands. We hope you enjoy it.

—Roxanne

ACKNOWLEDGEMENTS

I have to credit the inspiration for this book to my longtime friend Davonna Wallace. Without her putting the idea into my head for a book about Flint's haunted locations, *Haunted Flint* would not exist. I would never have taken my love of Flint history and combined it with all the urban legends and local ghost stories that I had been collecting and put them into a detailed book. I also want to thank all the local historians who helped me find details, dates, ghost stories and images for the book, including Flint author Gary Flinn, historian Daniel Conner, and all those who submitted their personal ghost stories. And a huge thank-you to my coauthor, Joe Schipani, who is the research master.

—Roxanne

This book was inspired by the many great people of Flint who have shared their stories and experiences and by many long years of research at the Flint Public Library. I would like to thank all the librarians who have answered my questions, guided me in the right direction and put away all the microfilm rolls I used. The Flint Public Library is truly one of the city's most valuable assets. I would like to thank the owner and staff of Totem Books in Flint for letting me camp out there and use the store as an office away from home. And I can't forget the people who have encouraged me along the way. Ashley, Jessica, Pam, Angela and Jessie—thank you.

—Joe

INTRODUCTION

In a world where nearly every moment of our lives is photographed, recorded, and documented, the gaps in the past still beckon us. Searching for ghosts can be an attempt to reconstruct what is lost. By sifting through time for stories that have been misplaced or forgotten, we listen to the voices that call out to be remembered.
—*Colin Dickey*, Ghostland

Shadows lurking in corners, voices in the middle of the night, cold spots sending shivers up and down your spine…

Every city has ghosts, some more than others. Places that have seen battles, horrible disasters and deadly histories are reported to be the most haunted. Such pain and suffering are sure to leave a mark. From feelings of unease to reports of spooky specters and terrifying encounters—the stories of hauntings are sometimes scarier than the history that created the ghosts. These cities are often considered to be America's most haunted: New Orleans, Louisiana; San Francisco, California; Savannah, Georgia; Chicago, Illinois; Washington, D.C.; Portland, Oregon; Gettysburg, Pennsylvania; Galveston, Texas; Baltimore, Maryland; Salem, Massachusetts; and Charlotte, North Carolina. All these cities have seen their share of disasters, battles and shady dealings. They are also large, well-known cities that are popular travel destinations.

Flint, Michigan, isn't large and it sure isn't a tourist destination, but it has an extensive history of pain, suffering, crime, hardship and…ghost stories.

The Travel Channel's paranormal television show *The Dead Files* has filmed three episodes in Flint. *The Dead Files* features two paranormal investigators: psychic medium Amy Allan and former NYPD homicide detective Steve DiSchiavi. They travel the country investigating paranormal activity. Amy has felt more than human spirits on the properties they've investigated in Flint; she's also encountered elementals and demonic entities.

Flint is home to ancient Native American battle sites and burial grounds, the Sit-Down Strike of 1936–37, unsolved murders, economic depression, social injustice, devastating floods, a deadly tornado and a water crisis. This unholy brew of energy has led to freaky tales of ghostly encounters and demonic possession.

What is to blame for all these strange occurrences? Is there something sinister lurking in Flint's history to blame for all the hauntings? Is the land truly cursed by the spirits of the Sauks, a Native American tribe whose members were massacred here?

Or perhaps it is the high crime rate. Flint has numerous murders every year, many unsolved. Do the souls of the murdered linger, craving justice by haunting the land until they get their vengeance?

Whatever the reason, Flint is filled with frightful sites and terrifying tales.

From ghostly graveyard apparitions in Glenwood and Sunset Hills to spooky specters spotted in downtown Flint's Capitol Theatre and the Whiting, Flint is filled with ghosts.

1

FLINT IS A GHOST TOWN

THE EARLY YEARS

Could secrets hidden in the history of Flint's founding father be the source of some of the city's troubles? Did his misdeeds leave a stain on the very fabric this city was built on?

Jacob Smith's story starts in Quebec, where he was born in 1773 to a Canadian soap maker of German descent, John Rudolf Smith.

The memory of Jacob Smith is both obscure and romanticized. Stories abound of his deeds; some are completely fictionalized, while others hold a hint of accuracy.

Historian Kim Crawford dug deep into historical records to find the truth about Flint founder Jacob Smith. His book *The Daring Trader: Jacob Smith in the Michigan Territory, 1802–1825* paints a picture of an enigma, creating as many questions as he answers, showcasing a man both self-serving and heroic. He was a man who cared deeply for the Native Americans even while helping the U.S. government take their land.

Some men claim Smith was a rascal of dubious nature; others thought him to be a very good man to know in the wilds of Michigan. Stories of his heroic actions during the War of 1812 are many. It is said he risked his own life and fortune on behalf of his adopted country and that he continued to secretly serve his country for many years after the war.

Not much can be found about his early life before leaving Quebec. Jacob married Mary Reed in 1798 and worked as a butcher before leaving Canada. Sometime between 1799 and 1801, he became a fur trader. Records show him in the Detroit area around 1800.

Smith, already fluent in French, German and English, became fluent in the Chippewa-Ottawa dialect of the Algonquin language and forged a skill of fostering positive relationships with the Native Americans. Sometime around 1811, he established a trading post at the Grand Traverse, the southernmost point of the Flint River. He was the first white citizen to farm on the Flint River, thanks to his close relationships with the Chippewa.

> *In 1811, Smith's trading post alongside the Flint River was the beginning of one of the nation's most resilient and inspiring cities. The City of Flint has enjoyed both triumph and misery. It has gone from a shining example of what the United States can be, to a tragic example of what it could become, to the icon of perseverance and pride that it is today. The city has produced heroes of commerce, business, manufacturing, solidarity, athletics, the arts, and philanthropy. Flint's fortune has ebbed and flowed like that of its namesake and like its namesake, it is forever moving forward, unstoppable. Since 1811, Flint has been a great piece of the fabric of our nation.* [Peter Hinterman, "Flint through the Decades"]

Smith fought in the War of 1812 and ingratiated himself with powerful men, like Lewis Cass, who became the territorial governor after the war ended. During the war, Smith worked as an intelligence gatherer, confidential agent and Indian interpreter-liaison. This work was unofficial yet acknowledged by Cass. Smith's good relations with the Chippewa helped him become close to Chief Neome. The Chippewa "adopted" him and gave him the name Wahbesins, "Young Swan." (On his gravestone in Glenwood, it is spelled "Wah-be-seens.")

Thanks to Smith's ties to both the native tribes and the white men in power, he played a major role in negotiating the treaty of 1819. The Saginaw Cession and Treaty ceded over six million acres of land to the U.S. government. A large piece of that land was located along the Flint River.

In addition to being on the government payroll, "Smith also carved out his own personal reward in the treaty, pulling off a real estate sleight of hand that makes all disreputable land speculators in present-day Flint look like amateurs" (Gordon Young, *Tear Down*, 39).

"The audacity of Jacob Smith at the Treaty of Saginaw was truly impressive. On one hand, he was acting as a secret agent on behalf of Cass to get the Chippewa and Ottawa to approve the cession of a huge portion of Michigan's Lower Peninsula. At the same time, he was also laying groundwork for his children to claim and eventually receive thousands of acres of land by getting Indian names for them into the treaty." (Kim Crawford, *Daring Trader*)

The treaty reserved large tracts of land for several white and mixed-blood Native Americans. Each was to receive 640 acres. Jacob Smith used his role as a negotiator to get portions of the land into the hands of friends and family members who were given Chippewa names, including five of his children. Some say Smith claimed that his wife, Mary, was Chippewa (Ojibwa), while many historians say she was a Canadian of Irish descent. Eventually, there were battles over the land, as many people tried to claim they were actually the Chippewa named in the treaty. Legal battles went on for years; in the end, Smith's heirs held on to the land.

Some argue that the tribes wanted Smith to have the land, that his relationship with the tribes secured their favor: "It is safe to say, that of the 114 chiefs and head men of the Chippewa nation, whose totems were affixed to the treaty, there was not one with whom he had not dealt and to whom he had not extended some act of friendship, either dispensing the rights of hospitality at his trading post, or in substantial advances to them of bread or blankets, as their necessity required." (F.C. Bald, Detroit's First American Decade)

There are others who say Jacob Smith used underhanded means when negotiating the treaty, like getting the Chippewa drunk and forcing them to sign. If this is true, it really is a black mark on Flint's history, a dark stain that seeped deep into the very foundation this city was built on. But the truth is lost in history, and what remains is highly subjective.

Author Kim Crawford's *Daring Trader* digs deep into Smith's life and finally gives us a detailed and more accurate view of Jacob Smith. But even it doesn't give us all the answers: "Bold and controversial, self-serving and sacrificing, mercenary and patriotic, Jacob Smith served Michigan's first two territorial governors as translator, soldier, courier and confidential agent among the Saginaw Chippewa and Ottawa Indians."

"Smith won no battles or blazed new trails; he was not even an official party, signatory, or witness to the 1819 treaty he helped the federal government win from the Indian leaders. Yet no other fur trader in the Michigan Territory had the sort of influence he did" (Kim Crawford, *Daring Trader*).

Smith was a controversial figure in both life and death. He died in obscurity in 1825. None of his children came to care for him when he was sick; at the end, he was attended only by Jack, a young Indian man Smith had adopted. Several Indians attended his burial, including Chief Neome, who was filled with grief on losing his friend.

When he died, Smith left behind debt and an uncertain legacy for his heirs. Lawsuits that had plagued him in life continued to plague his heirs. He made many reckless business decisions and had a stack of unpaid debts. The land he won for his children in the treaty was disputed, and their resolution of the dispute dragged through the courts for decades.

After Smith died, his son-in-law Chauncey S. Payne came and removed all his belongings from the cabin and left it abandoned. Smith's estate was divided up and given to his creditors to pay his debts. Flint's first permanent structure, built by Flint's first speculator and failed businessman, became its first abandoned building.

Smith was buried on his land next to his cabin by Baptiste Cochios, a mixed-blood trader. Smith was later reburied in Glenwood Cemetery with his daughters and sons-in-law, the Stocktons and Paynes.

The site where Smith's cabin stood is now a recognized State of Michigan historical marker. It is located near the corner of West First Avenue and Lyon Avenue in Carriage Town.

In 1873, Smith's daughter Louisa Payne and her husband, Chauncey, donated the site to the First Baptist Church of Flint. She had received the land through the treaty. The First Baptist Church resided on the site from 1873 to 1889.

Around 1892, Stephen Crocker built five houses in the area, including a Queen Anne Victorian home, which still stands on the site.

Fred Aldrich (1861–1957) moved into the Queen Anne house in 1894. A native of Van Buren County, Aldrich came to Flint when his father purchased the *Flint Globe* newspaper. Aldrich established the *Otter Lake Enterprise* newspaper in northeast Genesee County in 1880. He began working for his childhood friend William "Billy" C. Durant as a clerk at the Flint

Jacob Smith's grave in Glenwood Cemetery. *Courtesy of Ari Napolitano.*

18

Road Cart Company in 1889. He became secretary of the Durant-Dort Carriage Company on its incorporation in 1896. As a banker, Aldrich was instrumental in building the Durant and Flint Tavern Hotels.

Some of Flint's most haunting tales have connections to the locations and people tied to those pieces of land from the treaty, including a house located in Section Five of what is known as the old Smith Reservation. The Travel Channel's *The Dead Files* investigated the location in an episode that aired in June 2013 titled "Battlefield." The home was filled with spirits and possibly a demon. *The Dead Files* team performed an exorcism on the mother living in the home.

Another haunting tie is the Stockton Center at Spring Grove, considered to be Flint's most haunted location. The house was built by Colonel Thomas Stockton and his wife, Maria, who was the youngest daughter of Jacob Smith. Learn more about Stockton in chapter 6.

After Jacob Smith

Flint continued to grow and prosper after Smith's death. In 1835, the Village of Flint began with just over fifty-four acres. In 1855, the small but prosperous village officially became a city with around two hundred residents.

By the end of the nineteenth century, Flint was the center of Michigan's lumber industry. It had reached its peak as a lumbering town in 1870 with eighteen lumber dealers, eleven sawmills, nine planing mills, a box-making factory and a dealer in pine lands. As the lumber industry boomed, the next industry emerged: transportation. Carts, wagons and carriages were needed for transporting lumber, as well as lumber workers and their families.

In 1869, the first major carriage factory opened. Incorporated in 1896, the W.A. Paterson Company grew into a three-building complex along Saginaw and Harrison Streets.

In the early 1880s, as the lumber industry faded, Flint Wagon Works was founded. James H. Whiting, manager of the Begole Fox lumber business, suggested the company make wagons. He partnered with Josiah W. Begole, David S. Fox, George L. Walker and Allen Beach Sr. and set up shop on Flint's West Kearsley Street in a vacant Begole Fox lumberyard.

Josiah Dallas Dort and Billy Durant bought the Coldwater Cart Company in 1886 and moved it to Flint, renaming it the Flint Road Cart Company.

W. A. PATERSON'S PLANT.

A drawing of the Paterson Factory. *From the book* Headlight Flashes along the Grand Trunk Railway System; Flint, Michigan.

In 1895, it was renamed the Durant-Dort Carriage Company. These three carriage companies became the original "Big Three."

In 1899, seven wrought-iron arches were erected to illuminate the Downtown Flint business district. The electric arches replaced gas lanterns. Flint, ever the source of innovation at the time, was one of the first cities to light up its streets in such a manner. Built by Genesee Iron Works, each arch held no fewer than fifty light bulbs. During holidays and parades, the arches were adorned with festive decorations.

Business was booming, and men from all over the United States came to Flint for manufacturing jobs. By 1900, Flint was producing more than 100,000 horse-drawn vehicles per year. In the early twentieth century, Flint became a successful automobile manufacturing city.

Judge Charles Wisner, a genius who patented five inventions and whose workshop still stands in the historic Crossroads Village, drove Flint's first horseless carriage down Saginaw Street in the Labor Day Parade in 1900. The carriage moved like magic, wowing approximately ten thousand spectators before it eventually stuttered and stalled. But that ride lasted long enough to catch the eye of Billy Durant. Durant did not buy Wisner's patent for the automobile, but the idea of a horseless carriage stuck in his head.

A drawing of the Durant-Dort Carriage Company. *From the book* Headlight Flashes along the Grand Trunk Railway System; Flint, Michigan.

In 1901, the Durant-Dort Carriage Company was the second business to plug into electricity, right behind the *Flint Daily Globe* newspaper. This completely changed the manufacturing industry.

Flint Wagon Works, a rival of Durant and Dort, pushed the city fully into the automobile craze in late 1903. President James H. Whiting made the decision to purchase David Buick's fledgling Buick Motor Company to build engines for farm equipment. David Dunbar Buick and his chief engineer, Walter Marr, stayed with the company and convinced Whiting to manufacture the first Buick motorcar. In 1904, Flint Wagon Works had begun producing automobiles, but it was slow and costly. Whiting was frustrated. He dissolved the old Buick Motor Company and incorporated a completely new entity, the Buick Motor Company. Billy Durant then took over management of Buick.

In June 1905, Flint celebrated its fiftieth birthday with a golden jubilee celebration. Floats paraded down Saginaw Street depicting the evolution of the vehicle; buildings were dressed in red, white and blue buntings and flags; and two additional arches were added. These new arches featured the Vehicle City crown at their apex. As stated in the program of the Golden Jubilee of Flint 1905:

It is made known to the state that Flint is a city of high ideals, that it is ambitious not only to take a leading place in the industrial and commercial world, but that it is seeking to develop and foster a higher type of intellectual, moral and patriotic citizenship, that it is endeavoring to establish and perpetuate institutions and influences alongside of its industrial and commercial enterprises that will preserve and strengthen its reputation of a city of homes, schools, and churches. It thus drew the attention of the best class of men and women, the kind who make a city prosperous in the highest sense.

The city of Flint officially became known as the "Vehicle City," though the moniker had been floating around locally for a few years thanks to the success of the carriage companies.

Josiah Dallas Dort had taken interest in building Flint's first park system. Eventually, 115 acres were designated as parkland within the City of Flint. While Dort was busy building parks in the city, Durant started luring Charles Stewart Mott to Flint. Mott was the president of the Weston-Mott Company in New York. Durant's charm worked, and in 1907, Mott moved his company to Flint and merged with the Buick Motor Company. During this time, the

Postcard featuring an early image of a Vehicle City arch. *Author collection.*

auto industry was booming and everyone was coming to try their hand at motorized fortune.

In 1908, Durant wanted to get a jump on the competition. He founded General Motors in Flint so he would be able to consolidate all the companies under one umbrella. He then acquired Oldsmobile, Cadillac, Oakland (which became Pontiac) and various truck companies that were all merged in GMC. He also purchased A.C. Sparkplug and moved it from Boston to Flint.

In 1908, Paterson joined the craze and began building the Paterson Automobile.

Durant got into a financial bind in 1910 and had to turn General Motors over to the banks because he was overextended. But that didn't stop him. He teamed up with racecar driver Louis Chevrolet to form the Chevrolet Motor Company in 1911. That year, the Dalton Automobile Company was started by Huber Dalton.

Ever the entrepreneur, Billy Durant added more companies to his resume in 1914 when he formed the Monroe Motor Company with R.F. Monroe from Pontiac. Both Monroe and Chevrolet vehicles were manufactured in the Chevrolet factory. Vehicle City was now cranking out Buick, Chevrolet, Paterson, Dalton, Wey, Whiting and Monroe automobiles in addition to trucks and carriages.

People were coming from all over the world to work in the factories and seek success. One immigrant quickly made his mark on Flint. Albert Koegel had learned meat-cutting and -processing techniques in his native Germany. He arrived in Flint and set up Koegel Meat Company on Kearsley Street. His success was immediate. To this day, Koegel is still one of the most successful businesses in the Flint area.

Thanks to Chevrolet's popularity, Durant was able to take back control of GM in 1916. In 1919, Durant hired Alfred P. Sloan and Charles F. Kettering to manage GM. The city was celebrating its centennial and Home Festival in honor of Jacob Smith.

Flint continued to see prosperity and growth, so much so that the famous arches were removed and traffic lights installed. (In 2002, under the watchful eyes of the Genesee County Historical Society, new arches were erected along Saginaw Street that replicated the originals.)

But Durant's success was on a downward slope. In 1920, he lost GM for the final time. He founded Durant Motors in 1921 and built a huge factory on South Saginaw Street between Atherton and Hemphill. Durant Motors folded in 1931, and Durant went bankrupt in 1936. The factory was sold

Postcard featuring the Vehicle City arches at Detroit Street. *Daniel Conner personal collection.*

to GM. This site became known as the Fisher Body Plant No. 1 and made bodies for Buick.

When the Fisher plant closed in 1987, it was a major blow to Flint's economy and started a downward spiral Flint has never recovered from. Michael Moore made a documentary film about it, *Roger & Me.*

THE FALL OF FLINT

For almost a century, Flint was a successful vehicle manufacturing area, businesses thrived and the economy was good. People came to Flint for work. By the 1920s, there were so many people coming to Flint that the housing market couldn't keep up. People slept in makeshift shacks along the river because there wasn't enough housing for all the workers. What follows is a summary of Flint's downfall.

The Sit-Down Strike of 1936–37 started an era of labor unions.

During World War II, Flint was a major contributor of tanks and other war machines, thanks to all the manufacturing facilities. Flint was a prominent city built around the automobile industry.

Postcard featuring a 1950s view of Saginaw Street. *Author collection.*

In the 1950s, Flint had one of the highest median incomes in the United States, as well as the highest rate of home ownership.

GM's U.S. employment peaked at 618,365 in 1979, making it the largest private employer in the United States. The city's population reached 200,000 by the 1960s. At its height, GM employed around 85,000 people in plants throughout the city. By the late 1980s, that started to change. The first major closure was the Fisher Body Plant in 1987.

The 1990s showcased a city trying desperately to hold on as it slid into economic despair. Buick headquarters moved from Flint to Detroit in 1998. In 1999, the Buick City Complex closed. In 2002, it was demolished.

Throughout the 2000s, many remaining factories in the area were closed. By July 2008, only around 7,100 GM jobs remained in the Flint area. By 2014, estimates indicate that at least half the population had left. Fewer than 100,000 people remained within the city limits, and 40 percent of them lived below the national poverty line.

Exodus of Residents

The closure of factories created a devastating ripple effect throughout the Flint area. After GM manufacturing facilities closed, all the small factories not owned by GM but that supplied parts to the auto company started closing. Following factory closures, gas stations, convenience stores and restaurants located around the factories shuttered, as they no longer had customers.

With no jobs available, people left the Flint area by the thousands. This exodus continued for decades.

In 2017, census numbers listed only 96,448 residents in Flint, less than half the number of Flint's high of 200,000. Between 2009 and 2013, approximately 41.5 percent of Flint's residents lived below the poverty line. A quarter had an annual income below $15,000. The city's child poverty rate was 66.5 percent.

As a result, empty houses and businesses are everywhere. You can't drive a block without seeing a building boarded up. There are neighborhoods that are complete ghost towns. The City of Flint was finally forced to do something about the empty houses, which had become dangerous. It started razing them. Between 2013 and 2015, around two thousand blighted and decaying homes were demolished by the City of Flint. Since 2005, over five thousand homes have been demolished. That is an extremely large number for a very small city.

Empty and boarded-up buildings are not just hot spots for vandals and criminals. They also spark the imagination. Urban legends and creepy tales flourish in the decay. Every boarded-up and abandoned building is a shell of what it once was. Whispers of hauntings start to surface. What inhabits these sad places once the living have moved on?

Urban Decay

At one time, the Flint school system had groundbreaking ideas. It was the national model for growing cities that were being fueled by the boom of American manufacturing.

But when the manufacturing jobs left, so did the residents. Without enough children in the area or tax-paying residents to fund local education, schools began closing. By 2014, twenty Flint Community Schools had closed, double the number of schools in the district that remained open.

Flint Central High School vandalized. *Courtesy of Ari Napolitano.*

In October 2015, the school district had two dozen buildings that had become hot spots for vandalism, arson, drug violations and other crimes. The 911 system received at least one call per day regarding one of the empty buildings. There were more than forty-nine calls regarding shots fired at one of the locations. But the school district had no funds to properly maintain the locations or provide security.

Northwestern High School closed its doors in June 2018. Northwestern was one of the more successful schools in the Flint district, especially when it came to athletics. Many famous athletes graduated from Northwestern, including Olympic champion Claressa Shields and professional athletes Jeff Grayer, Glen Rice and Andre Rison.

Only one high school remains in the Flint Community School District: Flint Southwestern Classical Academy. The empty schools continue to decay, falling into ruin. The only economical option left is to tear them down, like the thousands of homes that have been demolished in Flint.

CRIME

A cash-strapped city cuts costs—one major cut was to the police force. Flint went broke and could no longer afford its police. To save money, the city

Flint Central High School crumbling. *Courtesy of Ari Napolitano.*

shuttered its police academy and cut its police force in half. Crime more than doubled.

A Netflix documentary, *Flint Town*, showcases the police force and its daily struggles. A headline from 2017 reads, "Flint Tries to Hire Police with Pay Less than Janitors, Manicurists, and Bellhops." The starting pay was $11.25 an hour, the equivalent of a $23,400 annual salary to risk one's life in one of the deadliest cities in America.

According to 2017 FBI statistics, Flint has the sixth-highest rate of violent crime in the United States, with 973 violent crimes reported per 50,000 residents.

For the year 2017, Flint crimes reported to the FBI included 1,879 violent crimes with 37 homicides, 104 rapes, 272 robberies and 1,466 assaults. The city's assault rate is among the highest in the nation. FBI figures show a person is more likely to be a victim of a felonious assault in Flint than in any other city with more than 50,000 people.

In a report published by the National Council for Home Safety and Security, "Top 100 Most Dangerous Cities of America in 2018," Flint came in fifth, with a rate of 2,109 violent crimes per 100,000 people. Flint was ranked as the most dangerous city that had fewer than 100,000 residents.

As of June 2018, Flint was *USA Today*'s second-worst U.S. city to live in. (Detroit is number one.)

WATER CRISIS

In addition to the crime rates, Flint has made headlines worldwide due to the water crisis. What many people don't know is that circumstances in the mid-twentieth century actually paved the disastrous road that led to the current problems.

It started in the mid-1950s, when concern arose that the Flint River could not meet the needs of a growing city. Claude O. Darby Sr., a confidential land agent for the city, recommended that Flint purchase land along Lake Huron to be used as a water pumping station.

Flint businessman Samuel M. Catsman, who owned local real estate and coal, fuel oil and concrete companies, was charged with cheating the City of Flint by using inside information about the planned pipeline route. He bought and sold the land at a huge markup. He was indicted for fraud. The scandal also included the arrest of former Flint city manager Robert A. Carter. The indictment of Catsman ended with the charges dismissed and the profit repaid to the city. (Read about the Catsman House in chapter 16.)

Within six months of the indictments, the city abandoned the pipeline project and, on June 6, 1964, signed a contract to buy water from the city of Detroit for the next thirty years.

In 2002, the Genesee County Board of Commissioners paid $2.73 million for 236 acres of Sanilac County property, including beachfront property on Lake Huron, in Worth Township—the same township where Flint purchased a much smaller parcel in January 1962.

The twenty-first-century crisis started in 2012, when Genesee County announced a new pipeline designed to deliver water from Lake Huron to Flint. The plan was going to reduce costs by switching the city's water supplier from the Detroit Water and Sewerage Department (DWSD) to the Karegnondi Water Authority (KWA). But instead of waiting for the KWA to be complete, Flint's water supply started coming from the Flint River. The switch occurred in April 2014. In August, a boil advisory was issued after fecal coliform bacterium was found in the water. Another boil advisory was issued in September 2014 after a positive test for total coliform bacteria.

In October 2014, the Michigan Department of Environmental Quality (MDEQ) issued a governor's briefing listing possible causes for the contamination issues, including leaking valves and aging cast-iron pipes. Also in October, the General Motors plant in Flint stopped using the city's water because it corroded engine parts. The company started purchasing water from Lake Huron.

In January 2015, residents were warned that the water contained by-products of disinfectants that may cause health issues, including an increased risk for cancer. The DWSD offered to reconnect the city with Lake Huron water, waiving a $4 million fee to restore service. City officials declined. Residents toted jugs of discolored water to a community forum. Local newspapers started reporting that Flint children were developing rashes and suffering from mysterious illnesses.

In February 2015, the MDEQ noted buildup of TTHM, a cancer-causing by-product of chlorine and organic matter. On February 26, the EPA notified the MDEQ it had detected dangerous levels of lead in the water at the home of Flint resident Lee-Anne Walters. Walters, a mother of four, contacted the EPA with concerns about dark sediment in her tap water. Testing revealed that her water had 104 parts per billion (ppb) of lead. That was nearly seven times greater than the EPA limit of 15 ppb.

In March 2015, another test by the EPA indicated the lead level in Walters's water had gone up to 397 ppb. On March 23, the Flint City Council members voted seven to one to stop using the Flint River and to reconnect with Detroit. State-appointed emergency manager Jerry Ambrose overruled the vote.

On June 24, 2015, an EPA manager issued a memo, "High Lead Levels in Flint." According to the memo, scientists at Virginia Tech tested tap water from Walters's home and found the lead level was as high as 13,200 ppb. Water contaminated with 5,000 ppb of lead is classified by the EPA as hazardous waste. Three other homes also had high lead levels in the water, according to the memo. Walters shared the memo with an investigative reporter from the ACLU, Curt Guyette.

In July, the ACLU posted a video about the lead in Walters's water. The ACLU then leaked the EPA memo. An MDEQ spokesman tried to downplay the problem by saying that testing on 170 homes indicated that the problem was not widespread. By September and October, Flint had made national headlines after tests showed children with elevated lead levels in their blood. Testing revealed that numerous homes, businesses and schools had contaminated water.

In December, Flint declared a state of emergency. In January 2016, Governor Rick Snyder declared a state of emergency in Genesee County. The National Guard was mobilized to distribute bottled water. Numerous lawsuits were filed and criminal charges brought against state officials. In

April 2018, Governor Snyder ended water distribution in Flint, claiming clean water had been restored.

As of this writing, there are still homes that have not had their pipes replaced. They still do not have clean water.

If the first attempt to switch to water from Lake Huron would not have been corrupted by Catsman, would the current water crisis have ever happened?

2
A Curse on the Land

Native American Legends

What's in a name? Some believe everything. Words have meaning. Names hold power…and secrets.

The Native Americans called the river that runs through Flint *pewonigowink*, which translates to "the river of the flint" or "river of the fire stone." The Flint River has a rocky riverbed, but it isn't flint rock. So why was the river, and later the city, named Flint?

In several Native American legends, Flint is the twin brother to hero god Sky-Holder, also known as Nanabozho. The grandsons of Sky Woman, they are the major players in many Native American creation myths.

One Iroquois legend says that Sky Woman was so filled with grief at losing her daughter, Tekawerahkwa, during the birth of the twins Good Mind and Bad Mind (Flint), that she took her daughter's head and put it in the sky to create Grandmother Moon.

Another legend says that the mother of the twins became Mother Earth when they buried her. Even after death, she provided them with what they needed. From her head grew corn, beans and squash—the Three Sisters, the staple foods of the Iroquois diet. From her heart grew sacred tobacco, which is used to communicate with the Creator. From her feet grew wild strawberry, the Big Medicine.

All the legends agree that Flint killed his mother in childbirth. He was sharp and cold and cut his way out. Because of this, in many tribes, Flint is associated with winter, night and death—the same symbols that could be used to describe the city of Flint over the years.

Flint is often portrayed as an evil or trickster god. Think of the popular Norse legends of Loki and his hero brother, Thor.

In some myths, Flint is portrayed as a sociopathic villain who must be defeated by his hero brother. In other traditions, Flint is more of a trickster than a villain. It is simply his chaotic nature that brings about destruction, according to one Iroquois creation legend described on the website Native-Languages.org:

> *Sky Woman gave birth to twin sons. She named one Sapling. He grew to be kind and gentle. She named the other Flint and his heart was as cold as his name. They grew quickly and began filling the earth with their creations. Sapling created what is good. He made animals that are useful to humans. He made rivers that went two ways and into these, he put fish without bones. He made plants that people could eat easily. If he was able to do all the work himself there would be no suffering. Flint destroyed much of Sapling's work and created all that is bad. He made the rivers flow only in one direction. He put bones in fish and thorns on berry bushes. He created winter, but Sapling gave it life so that it could move to give way to Spring. He created monsters which his brother drove beneath the Earth.* [Lyndsey Murtaugh, "Iroquois Creation Myth," Common Elements in Creation Myths (https://www.cs.williams.edu/~lindsey/myths/myths.html]

Could the river and city have been named Flint because something dark, chaotic and otherworldly resides in the depths of the land?

NATIVE AMERICAN BURIAL GROUNDS

A familiar tale of hauntings—especially for horror movie tropes—is the Native American burial ground. Disturbing the spirits is never a good idea, even if you do it by accident. Anyone remember the terrifying 1980s movie *Poltergeist*?

Numerous construction sites in Flint have unearthed ancient remains. Historical records indicate that Flint is soaked with the blood of a battle so epic it has long been considered just myth and legend. But in recent years, native remains and artifacts have lent legitimacy to the old legends.

One version of the tale claims that, around 1600, the Sauk traveled from the St. Lawrence River region in the state of New York to the Saginaw Bay area of Michigan. They settled throughout the region between Bay City and Detroit. For years, the Sauk prospered on the rich and fertile lands, where game to hunt was plentiful.

The Ojibwa (commonly known in Michigan as Chippewa) inhabited the lands north of Saginaw Bay. These lands were harsh, due to the northern climate; hunting and farming were difficult. The Ottawa resided in Canadian regions and the Lake Huron area.

Around the years 1638–40, the Ojibwa and Ottawa became interested in the lands of the Sauk. The tribes banded together and invaded lower Michigan, including the area of Flint, and massacred the Sauk. They entered the Sauk region in a coordinated plan of attack. The Ottawa came through the woods from the Detroit area, and the Ojibwa traveled by night in canoes.

Half of the Ojibwa canoe force landed at the mouth of the Saginaw River, while the others traveled across the bay. The two groups stealthily worked their way along each side of the river and attacked their unsuspecting prey. Survivors were driven across the Saginaw River to another village, where they encountered more warriors.

Some escaped to a small island. They thought themselves safe, because the enemy had no canoes in the river. But the water froze, and the warriors were able to cross the ice to the island, where another bloody massacre took place. The island was so thickly strewn with bones and skulls that it later became known as Skull Island.

The Ojibwa continued their bloody rampage through villages on the Shiawassee, Tittabawassee, Cass and Flint Rivers. The Ottawa forces came in from the south and struck the Flint River Sauk near the southernmost bend of the river. A deadly battle was fought on a bluff bank of the river about a half mile below the present city of Flint. The Sauk suffered a major defeat and retreated to an area now known as Flushing. Another bloody battle was fought, the results as disastrous as the first. Then another battle took place to the north around the area that today is the boundary of Genesee and Saginaw Counties. It was a devastating attack that almost completely eradicated the Sauk. The few Sauk who managed to escape took refuge in the wilderness near Lake Michigan. Eventually, they left Michigan altogether.

After the massacre, the Ojibwa and Ottawa divided up the lands and lived in peace. They did not take residence in these new lands but used them as hunting grounds. Then hunters started disappearing. It seemed normal; conditions are harsh, accidents happen and it isn't unusual for a few men to never return from a hunting trip. But the number of disappearances became alarming. Frightened whispers started. At first, tribe members thought some Sauk might still inhabit the hunting grounds and were taking revenge.

Then men came back terrified of what they encountered, and stories were told of the forests being "haunted by the spirits of the murdered Sauks, who had come back to their former hunting-grounds to take vengeance on their merciless destroyers." The terrors they encountered were not from any flesh-and-blood humans. *Manesous* (bad spirits) filled the forests.

Edwin Orin Wood, author of *History of Genesee County Michigan*, says, "These Indians were extremely superstitious and believed in evil spirits, especially the ghosts of the Sauks. Ephraim S. Williams, the Indian trader of Saginaw and Flint, tells of their fears as follows":

> *It has been mentioned that the ancient Chippewas imagined the country which they had wrested from the conquered Sauks to be haunted by the spirits of those whom they had slain, and that it was only the lapse of years that their terrors were sufficiently allayed to permit them to occupy the "haunted grounds." But the superstition still remained, and in fact it was never entirely dispelled. Long after the Saginaw valley was studded with white settlements, the simple Indian still believed that mysterious Sauks were lingering in their forests and along the margins of the streams for the purposes of vengeance; that "Manesous," or bad spirits in the form of Sauk warriors, were hovering around their villages and camps and the flanks of their hunting grounds, preventing them from being successful in the chase and bringing ill-fortune and discomfiture in a hundred ways. So great was their dread that when (as was frequently the case) they became possessed with the idea that the "Manesous" were in their immediate vicinity, they would fly as for their lives, abandoning everything—wigwams, fish, game and all their camp equipment.*

Do these spirits still haunt Flint? Angry ghosts wreaking havoc upon any who dare live here? With the bad luck that continues to befall Flint, I often wonder if this land is cursed.

Do the bones found in Flint belong to Chippewa ancestors or to the Sauk who were savagely killed? Have we stumbled upon sacred burial grounds or bones left on the battlefield? Have the spirits of the Sauk remained to destroy whoever wishes to reside in their homeland?

In June 1962, remains were uncovered by a grading crew at M-15 and Bristol Road in Flint. In 2009, the remains of an adult and child, thought to be the same ones found in 1962, were found in storage at Mott Community College. MCC turned them over to the Saginaw Chippewa Indian Tribe, which gave the skeletons a proper burial.

In 2008, skeletal remains found near Atwood Stadium at Stone Street and Third Avenue were determined to be Native American. Further excavation by archaeological teams determined that the remains were most likely Sauk from that bloody battle. In 2010, the remains of sixty-seven American Indian ancestors were laid to rest in a reburial at the same site.

Stories often imply that restless spirits can be appeased with proper blessings and burials, but even after those bones were properly laid to rest, things haven't improved in Flint.

Are there more bones hiding under homes and businesses in Flint? More burial grounds waiting to be unearthed? Do the Sauk still seek revenge on those who trespass on their land?

3

A Haunting on the Hill

A Mansion with Murderous History

A haunted house is a memory palace made real: a physical space that retains memories that might otherwise be forgotten, or which might remain only in fragments. Under the invisible weight of these memories, the habits of those who once haunted these places, we feel the shudder of the ghost.
—*Colin Dickey,* Ghostland

A beautiful Georgian colonial in a ritzy Flint subdivision known as Knob Hill has quite a haunting history. The home was built in 1916 by Flint mayor George Kellar. The beautiful, three-story Georgian colonial home stands tall in the classy Knob Hill neighborhood across from the Michigan School of the Deaf and Powers Catholic High School.

The brick-exterior home features oak, maple and Douglas fir furnishings, chandeliers imported from Italy and France and soapstone sinks. This gorgeous mansion even has a ballroom in the basement. The home also features a butler's pantry and widow's walk.

The first owner, George Kellar, was mayor of Flint in 1917 and served a one-year term. He was followed as mayor by Charles Stewart Mott in 1918. In 1919, Kellar served another one-year term. The home was later purchased by Grace MacDonald, widow of Flint mayor Bruce J. MacDonald, who had served in 1904. Socialite Grace MacDonald was the first president of Flint's YWCA. She was a suffragist and very active in the women's voting movement.

In the late twentieth century, the home was bought and sold several times.

Despite the house's grisly history, former owners Samuel A. Ragnone and Dr. Vladimir Schwartsman adored the architecture of the home and coexisted with the ghosts of Crescent Drive during their separate times in the mansion. They say it added to the mystique and uniqueness of the place. "It didn't bother me to live there at all. In fact, I enjoyed the little-added suspense that it gave you. It made some people uncomfortable, but it was always fun," said Ragnone in an interview that appeared in the *Flint Journal*.

Ragnone enjoyed the eerie atmosphere, which made his Halloween parties a huge success. "I threw a great Halloween party there one night," he said. "There were a couple of hundred people there. The house was totally decorated, and it was just awesome."

But one time, things got to be too much, even for him. Doors slamming, strange noises. Ragnone reported that, one night, the noises became so loud that the police were called, but nothing and no one was found. The haunts are thought to be tied to a grisly murder that occurred on the site and to the home's close ties to another murder. Both murders involved women who were killed by their sons.

Things first turned ugly in this beautiful home in 1933, when Grace MacDonald was bludgeoned to death by her seventeen-year-old son, Balfe, in her upstairs bedroom. This blood-chilling scenario was repeated forty-six years later, after Helen Wirsing purchased the house. She never had the chance to move into the home, as she was shot to death by her twenty-year-old son, Mark, and buried outside of their cottage in Holly.

The first murder occurred in the early-morning hours of May 27, 1933. Grace MacDonald went to her bedroom, where she was packed and ready to go to the family's lake house for the summer. Mrs. Flower, the household maid, reported that Grace's son, Balfe, followed her to her room. He wanted to talk to her.

Balfe was a troubled boy. He ran with an unsavory crowd and was rumored to be a sadist. He and his mother were always at odds. She could not control him. At one point, she requested that he be locked up, and he spent two days in jail under the name "John Smith." Neighbors claimed to see and hear mother and son fighting all the time. He once chased her out of the house with a pistol. The day before the murder, Grace had an officer stop by to talk to Balfe about his behavior. She thought it might scare him straight. Instead, it seems to have made things worse.

When Mrs. Flower went to wake Grace in the morning, she found her on the floor in the midst of a disaster area. The room was a mess, filled with signs of struggle. When the police arrived, they found the murder weapon under a mess of pillows strewn about the room. Balfe MacDonald had viciously bashed his mother's head in with a pair of heavy onyx bookends from her shelf.

Balfe was nowhere to be found. Bloody clothes were found in Grace's bathroom, where he had undressed and bathed after the assault. But he was long gone.

A funeral took place in the Crescent Drive home, followed by Grace MacDonald's burial in Glenwood Cemetery. The pursuit of Balfe MacDonald went on for close to two weeks. He was finally apprehended in Tennessee a few days after the funeral. Balfe admitted to killing his mother but claimed that something in the house possessed him and forced him to do it. The newspapers painted him as a spoiled rich boy with mental problems.

The court dismissed his insanity pleas and his claim of being demonically possessed. He was charged with manslaughter and sentenced to ten to fifteen years in prison. He served only six years and was released in January 1940 at the age of twenty-three.

The house remained vacant for many years. In 1979, Helen Wirsing purchased the home, but she never had a chance to live there. It is thought that a couple of her children did reside in the home, including her son Mark.

On September 19, 1979, Helen Wirsing went missing. Her youngest child, twenty-year-old Mark, was immediately a suspect. The young man had mental issues and had recently spent two months in the Ypsilanti State Hospital after shooting his brother. The boy had assaulted his mother several times in the past, but she never wanted to press charges. However, she did make it known to those close to her that if anything ever happened to her, Mark was probably to blame.

Wirsing's body was not found for six months. In April 1980, Mark confessed to his sister that he killed their mother and buried her near their summer cottage in Holly. The location he provided was vague. It took days to locate it. Army reservists, Boy Scouts, tracking dogs and police joined the hunt to find her body.

Even though Mark Wirsing admitted to shooting his mother, he was found not guilty by reason of insanity.

Is it simply a coincidence that this house is connected to two mentally unstable young men who happened to murder their mothers? Or is there something dark lurking in this beautiful old home that makes young men murderous? Does this dark entity still linger among the shadows of the house, waiting for another young man to come along that it can influence?

4

Built on a Cemetery

The Holiday Inn Express

"Ghosts don't haunt us. That's not how it works. They're present among us because we won't let go of them."
"I don't believe in ghosts," I said, faintly.
"Some people can't see the color red. That doesn't mean it isn't there," she replied.
—Sue Grafton, M Is for Malice

A nother familiar ghost story trope, the "built on top of a cemetery" haunting, is one we see quite often. Many times, there is no factual basis for the rumors, but in the following case, the bones tell us a tale of being left behind when the cemetery was moved.

Old Flint City Cemetery was established in 1842 when Flint was still a village. It was located along southbound Chavez Drive and eastbound Longway Boulevard, meeting at the intersection of Avon Street, which is now W.H. Schwartz Drive. The cemetery contained some of the first settlers in Flint. Lack of maintenance left some graves unmarked or poorly marked, making it impossible to find all of the bodies when the city expanded in the turn of the twentieth century.

By the 1950s, the cemetery was overgrown and no one was taking care of it. The city decided to redevelop the area. Starting in 1952 1,199 residents of the Old Flint City Cemetery were disinterred and reburied at the new Flint City Cemetery on Linden Road and Pasadena Avenue. In 1958, the remaining residents of Old Flint City Cemetery, along with 122 grave markers, were moved to Avondale Cemetery. The area in the back of Avondale is called Pioneer's Row. But some bodies were left behind.

The Holiday Inn Express, built on top of an old cemetery. *Courtesy of Joe Schipani.*

In 1985, more than two dozen remains were found under the basement of the Holiday Inn Express (originally a Hampton Inn) at 1150 Longway Boulevard and I-475. The remains were reburied at the New City Cemetery.

Many people have reported strange occurrences and ghostly visions at the Holiday Inn. One common phenomenon at the location is a loss of power with no known cause. Lights go out, and electrical devices are suddenly drained of power. People hear voices and see shadowy figures walking the halls. One figure has been spotted quite often on the second floor. A former employee claims that doors would open and close by themselves and phone calls would come in to the front desk from empty rooms. But no words were ever spoken, and no one was found to be in the rooms making the calls.

Some believe the spirits left behind when the cemetery was relocated are trapped in the building.

5

A HAUNTED MANSION

THE WHALEY HOUSE

Haunted houses are the repository of the dreams dreamt inside them—both our dreams and those of previous occupants. This can make even the most simple of houses feel, at times, alive.
—Colin Dickey, Ghostland

The Whaley House, at 519 South Saginaw Street, started life in 1859 as an Italianate structure. Italianate architecture is based on rambling Italian countryside farmhouses. Its picturesque masonry structures are somewhat boxy in design yet feature ornate windows and doors. American examples of Italianate often mix details from both informal rural farmhouses and formal Renaissance townhouses.

The Italianate style was at the height of popularity in the pre–Civil War era and continued being one of the more popular forms of U.S. architecture through the 1870s. But by the late 1880s, the wealthy were building lavish Victorians.

Robert Jeremiah Whaley hired Detroit architect George Watkins to design an extensive Victorian remodel of the Italianate house. Victorian architecture showcases more intricate details and embellishment than does Italianate. The house was transformed from a boxy Italianate to an extravagant Victorian.

Robert J. Whaley and his wife, Mary (McFarlan) Whaley, moved into their home at 624 East Kearsley Street in 1885. The Whaley family consisted of Robert; Mary; their adopted daughter, Florence; and Robert's half-sister, Laura.

The exterior of the Victorian Whaley House Museum. *Courtesy of Ari Napolitano.*

Robert Whaley, president of Citizens Bank for over forty years, loaned Billy Durant $2,000 to start a road cart company that led to the creation of General Motors. Mary's father, Alexander McFarlan, was a businessman and former Flint mayor. After Robert Whaley died in 1922, she donated land to Flint that became the city's first park, McFarlan Park, in honor of her father.

The Whaleys' son, Donald, died at the age of ten from diphtheria. To help Mary overcome her grief, Robert encouraged her to memorialize their son. They set aside land and funds for the Whaley Children's Foundation to provide care for homeless and neglected children. This foundation still exists today and operates as Whaley Children's Center.

Mary passed away in 1925. Through her will, she also created the McFarlan Home for Women, directing that her estate take the residence at 624 East Kearsley Street and convert it into a home for elderly women and be named in honor of her parents. During its time as a home for elderly women, the home went through many remodels and renovations and housed numerous women until 1974, when the McFarlan Home built a much larger building next door, which is where it still operates, right next to the Whaley Historic House Museum.

In the mid-1970s, seven community organizations joined together to create the Whaley Historic Association. Major restoration transformed the home back to its Victorian-era charm so that it would look much like it did when the Whaleys lived there.

Whaley Historic House Museum has operated ever since. It is the place to visit at Christmas if you are interested in experiencing an authentic Victorian holiday. But you may be more interested in visiting during the Halloween season. That's when the Whaley House likes to showcase the eeriness of the manor.

Levitating tarps, moving toys, ringing bells, curtains blowing with no wind and shadowy figures fill this haunted mansion. In the basement, you may feel an unearthly chill and a sense of being watched. Throughout the old Victorian, many visitors have reported feeling a strong female presence along with the sensation of being unable to catch their breath.

Throughout the years, many Whaley staff and volunteers have had odd experiences in the house: seeing shadows out of the corner of their eyes,

Whaley House front parlor. *Courtesy of Ari Napolitano.*

rustling noises even though no one else is around and the odd sound of bells ringing. A former director was alone in the basement one day when a woman screamed right behind him. Terror propelled him up the stairs without ever turning around to see what it was.

The current director of the house has heard footsteps on the second floor, though he knew he was alone in the building. Several times he stopped what he was working on to investigate. But not another living soul was found.

Some claim that the children's room on the second floor is a hotbed of activity. Curtains move even though there is no air current, toys roll into the hallway and a rocking chair rocks as if an unseen child is moving it.

In 2014, the director of the Whaley House decided to embrace the Halloween season and offer a month of haunted history to the community. The month included a lecture, "Why Does the Nineteenth Century Seem So Creepy?," as well as a nineteenth-century séance, several historical tours and a sold-out ghost hunt.

Motor City Ghost Hunters caught electronic voice phenomena (EVP) in several rooms of the house and recorded strong electromagnetic field (EMF) readings in the basement. The team concluded that several members of the Whaley family still reside within the house. But not to worry—the spirits are friendly and won't harm anyone.

In November 2015, a fire broke out on the roof while a contractor was welding the copper gutters. The roof, the third-floor storage space, two bedrooms on the second floor, the music room and the main stairwell sustained extensive damage from fire, smoke and water, resulting in the home being closed for over two years for renovations. Several meaningful historic items were lost, along with several pieces of period furniture and many Christmas items. Items that could be preserved needed repair. Some of the home's original mantelpieces needed to be replaced.

One bright side to the fire was the opportunity to restore the home with more period-appropriate furnishings, including thick, hand-painted, era-specific wallpaper. Now when you walk into Whaley House, you truly are taking a step back in time. Every attention to detail was utilized when restoring this beautiful manor, from the stunning Victorian wallpaper to the intricate design of the wood floors, to the textured walls. The furnishings are either original to the home, items that belonged to the Whaley family or are period specific.

Whaley is fully furnished and decorated in Victorian luxury, including ornate woodwork, rich velvet-covered settees and furniture that is both sturdy yet delicate in appearance. The Whaley family's original dining-room

Whaley House staircase. *Courtesy of Ari Napolitano.*

Whaley dining room with original table. *Courtesy of Ari Napolitano.*

table and silver candlesticks fill the dining room, and paintings and photos of the family hang on the walls. You can feel the history as you walk through the building.

The exterior of Whaley House was fully restored by October 2017. The interior took a little longer, but by mid-2018, the Whaley House was once again fully operational for community enjoyment. The 2018 holiday season showcased a gorgeous Victorian home draped with holiday finery. The house was open on weekends in December for holiday tours, Santa visits and a Victorian tea.

The new director has plans to take advantage of the house's spooky appeal and is planning special events for the Halloween season.

It's a wonderful place to visit, whether you are a history buff, a fan of the Victorian era or a ghost hunter. It offers a unique experience for each. When you visit, take a moment to reach out and feel the history. If you are quiet and listen hard enough, you may hear the voices of the past whispering to you.

6

A HOUSE WITH HISTORY

STOCKTON CENTER AT SPRING GROVE

Ghosts bridge the past to the present; they speak across the seemingly insurmountable barriers of death and time, connecting us to what we thought was lost. They give us hope for a life beyond death, and because of this help us to cope with loss and grief. Their presence is the promise that we don't have to say goodbye to our loved ones right away, and…what was left undone in one's life might yet be finished by one's ghost.
—*Colin Dickey,* Ghostland

The Stockton Center at Spring Grove, 720 Ann Arbor Street, is a haunting example of Italianate architecture. The Italian-style architecture is as romantic as Gothic Revival, which was also popular in the late 1800s, but the floor plans are much more open and friendlier for larger families. Inspired by lavish rural homes in Italy, the Italianate was a smaller cousin to the Tuscan countryside's elaborate villas, not as ostentatious as the huge villas yet stylish enough for a new generation of homeowners. The Italianate style was quite popular for upper-middle-class families.

Just one glance at this gorgeous old home and you will feel the eeriness emanating from it. It looms large on the edge of downtown Flint, overlooking a natural spring. The original Italianate structure was added on to in the early 1900s, when it became a hospital. More space was added as the hospital continued to grow. These additions turned an ornate home into a hulking monster on a hill.

Stockton at Spring Grove. *Courtesy of Ari Napolitano.*

Step through the grand double front doors into the main hallway and you are immediately transported into the past. The home still features its original ornate windows, doors, trim and moldings. Such features are examples of intricate woodwork. To your left, a staircase takes you to the second floor. To the right, you enter a two-room front parlor that can be separated by huge folding doors. The rooms are filled with beautiful hardwood floors and large ornate windows.

Stockton House can seem barren compared to Whaley House, though the house itself is lavish in appearance, with high ceilings, gorgeous woodwork, ornate windows and unique curved doors. Only one section of the Italianate structure is fully furnished in period-specific furniture for the museum: a parlor and dining area. The front parlor has a few pieces of furniture but stays open for events like yoga, meditation and meetings. The rest of the museum area is in the hospital wing.

When first built, the home had two stories and fourteen rooms for the family, plus a servant's area and a workshop. It was described by the *Wolverine Citizen*, the local newspaper, in 1872 as "among the most stylish and spacious of the many handsome first-class houses in our city." It features airy rooms

Above: Stockton House's huge hospital addition. *Courtesy of Ari Napolitano.*

Left: Organ inside Stockton House. *Courtesy of Roxanne Rhoads.*

Main entrance hallway of Stockton House. *Courtesy of Roxanne Rhoads.*

with twelve-foot ceilings decorated with ornate plaster rosettes to anchor the lighting fixtures and hardwood floors of maple, cherry and oak.

The hospital is a stark contrast to the ornate Italianate. The three-story addition features long hallways full of doors, bare institutional walls and tile floors. Every now and then you'll see a glimpse of the past: an antique wheelchair, old hospital beds, a child-size hospital crib or a tiny rocking horse.

The house first belonged to Colonel Thomas Baylis Whitmarsh Stockton and his family. Stockton was born in Walton, New York, in 1805. At seventeen, he was appointed to the United States Military Academy and graduated in 1827. From 1836 to 1846, he worked as both a military officer and a civilian and served in the Corps of Topographical Engineers in the Great Lakes region, developing and improving roads and harbors. This brought him to Flint, where he met his wife, Maria, the youngest daughter of Flint founder Jacob Smith. Maria was born in Detroit in 1813.

Thomas rejoined the military in 1847 and led the First Michigan Volunteers in the Mexican-American War. In the Civil War, he formed Michigan's Sixteenth Infantry Regiment. He served as civil and military governor in Cordova, Mexico, until the end of the war in 1848. He then returned to Flint for a couple of years. He founded the Genesee County Agriculture Society in 1850 and held many of the early county fairs on the Stockton property. In 1852, he was swept up by the gold rush and moved to California for six years.

The family was back in Michigan when the Civil War broke out. Colonel Stockton received a commission from President Abraham Lincoln and organized an army regiment of Michigan volunteers. Stockton was captured during the war and sent to Libby Prison. He was released two months later in a prisoner exchange, being the nephew of General James Longstreet's wife. He retired from the military in 1863 but still spent his time recruiting for the Union army.

The Stocktons were a wealthy and influential Flint family. Maria Stockton had inherited a large amount of land from her father, Jacob Smith, along the river and creeks. Maria was the founder and first president of the Ladies' Library Association, which became Flint's first public library. The Stocktons donated twenty acres of land to what is now known as the Michigan School of the Deaf.

Stockton House at Spring Grove was built in 1872. Spring Grove acquired its name because of the perpetual spring located behind the house. Thomas and Maria lived in the home until their deaths. The Colonel passed away

Left: Colonel Stockton's grave in Glenwood Cemetery. *Courtesy of Ari Napolitano.*

Right: Maria Stockton's grave in Glenwood Cemetery. *Courtesy of Ari Napolitano.*

in 1890 and Maria in 1898. They are buried in Glenwood Cemetery. The building housed four generations of Stocktons.

In 1920, Thomas Stockton, their grandson, sold the property to the Archdiocese of Detroit, and it became the first site of Saint Joseph's Hospital in Flint. A hospital wing was added. St. Joseph's was operated by the Sisters of St. Joseph. The thirteen-thousand-square-foot home gave the hospital room for fifty-two beds, a small chapel on the second floor and an attic floor where the sisters lived. The house had a manual rope-and-pulley elevator for the convenience of transporting patients from floor to floor. This was later converted to a modern elevator.

The hospital quickly outgrew the house, where it operated until 1936. That year, the building became a nursing and convalescent home for the elderly. It operated for decades under different names, including Kith Haven Nursing Home, Cecelia Home for the Aged and Stockton House Home for the Aged, until 1996.

Over the years, there have been many celebrations of life and death inside the walls of the Stockton Center. The last recorded birth is believed to have been on December 22, 1935.

After the nursing home closed in 1996, the building sat vacant until 2002, when it was purchased by Flint architect Freeman Greer and his wife, Renee. The Greers have worked hard over the years at renovating and restoring the building and preserving the history of Stockton Center at Spring Grove. The hospital area was preserved and updated to fit modern code, while the home area was restored to its natural beauty. The linoleum that covered the original hardwood floors was restored, as was the beautiful antique banister, bringing the rich architectural detail back to life. It has been an ongoing project.

The house was designated as a Michigan Historical Site in 2005 and received a State Historical Marker. In 2009, the award-winning movie *Alleged* was filmed at Stockton House and at several other locations around Flint, including Crossroads Village. The movie is centered on the "Scopes Monkey Trial," which took place in Dayton, Tennessee, in 1925 and stars Brian Dennehy, Fred Thompson, Colm Meaney, Nathan West and Ashley Johnson.

The building now provides office and meeting space, a museum and space to hold special events. Stockton Center at Spring Grove is a great example of Flint history still being utilized by Flint residents. It is open to the public on selected dates for tours of the museum areas. Stockton often opens for parties at Halloween and Christmas. Rooms of the old hospital are rented as office space to local businesses. *Haunted Flint* coauthor Joe Schipani once had an office in the basement of the hospital wing.

Over the years, there have been many claims of haunting experiences in the home. Whistling, eerie footsteps and disembodied voices haunt the rooms of this old mansion. In addition to any number of patients who died at the site, both Colonel Stockton and Maria passed away in the house. On the evening of Maria's death, there reportedly was a terrible thunderstorm, and lightning struck the house. Several rafters in the attic still remain charred from the fire that was started by the lightning strike. Quite a bit of paranormal activity happens in the attic. The entry hallway and the second floor near the stairs are other areas where footsteps, whistling and whispered voices are often heard, even though no one is there.

When Joe had an office on the basement level, he would often hear footsteps on the floors above him, even though he knew no one else was in the building. He would go upstairs to check, just to make sure no one else was there, but he never found anyone lurking about.

Stockton House event coordinator Jacquie Richardson has had several spooky experiences during the ghost tours, but the eerie occurrences have never been malicious. A young boy is often seen, even though no children are part of the tour group. One night during a tour, someone heard a little boy introduce himself as Jonathan, and a psychic once had a feeling that a boy named Jonathan was looking for his toy train. She thinks "The Whistler" is the home's night watchman; he keeps an eye on the place when no one is there. Could Colonel Stockton still be guarding his home?

During the tours, EMF meters are used, and they beep quite frequently. Michigan Spirit Quest Paranormal Team has investigated the house several times. After their October 2017 visit, team member Steve Wood said in an interview with WSMH.com that Stockton is "one of the most active places we've ever been to." They experienced quite a few EVPs. Whispery voices, odd footsteps and whistling were picked up on the microphones. Once, the sound of heavy footsteps was recorded—"stomp, stomp, stomp," like the sound of military boots on the wood floors.

Jacquie thinks that the Stocktons are still enjoying their home. She imagines the Colonel standing at the mantel enjoying his pipe and Maria in the library reading her favorite books while the children play in the Civil War room. She feels that the spirits of the home are very welcoming.

The spirits of the hospital section of the building may not be as welcoming. Many claim that the former morgue on the first level is a frequent location of weird happenings and that the old operating room experiences intense otherworldly activity. However, a businesswoman who rents an office in the hospital section of Stockton says that some of the spirits that remain are nurses who worked there. They continue to serve even in death. They are helpful spirits that do not bother her at all, even when she is working alone in the building late into the night.

A local medium says that Stockton is a "mess of activity. The ghosts don't even try to hide. They are like neglected toddlers trying to get your attention. The spirits are very much lost in madness." After a bad experience in the basement, she refuses to go to the lower levels alone. When in other hospital areas, she tries to stay busy and focused so she can ignore the spirits that refuse to be quiet. No other location has ever given her as much trouble as Stockton House. At other locations, she is able to block the intrusive spirits, but the ghosts at Stockton are so loud that there is no blocking.

If you visit Stockton Center at Spring Grove, Jacquie warns that, before you leave, you must remember to tell the supernatural residents, "You will not follow me home."

7

A Ghostly Production

The Capitol Theatre

By far one of the most beautiful buildings in downtown Flint, the Capitol Theatre was conceived by J. Bradford Pengelly when he purchased the property in 1923. He then partnered with Walter S. Butterfield, owner of the W.S. Butterfield Theatres, to create the Flint Capitol Building Company in 1924.

The theater was designed by architect John Eberson, pioneer of atmospheric theater design. They began building the venue in April 1927. It was to house a theater, an arcade, stores, offices and a basement bowling alley.

The Capitol opened its doors at 140 East Second Street on January 19, 1928. It was the Butterfield Theatres chain's seventy-fourth venue. At the time, the Capitol Theatre was Flint's largest and Butterfield's most lavish, with its picturesque design and atmospheric elements, including cloud machines and lighting that depicted sunrise, sunset and twinkling stars. The atmosphere, combined with the Italian Renaissance design, transported theatergoers to the patio of an Italian garden under a Mediterranean sky.

The opening program began with this greeting:

Welcome to the Capitol Theatre, a touch of Italy transferred in its seductive charms to the City of Flint. Here ancient culture and art rub shoulders with the ultra-modern art of the cinema. With a heavy handclasp, we bid you a cordial welcome and trust that the hours spent within the shrine of entertainment will be the means of making your days more joyful. It will even be our purpose to provide the best in music, photoplays and stage presentations of the ultra in the field variety. [http://www.waymarking.com/waymarks/WM1HGG]

The twenty-five-thousand-square-foot building, with seating for two thousand, was the city's hot spot for movies for many decades. *Gone with the Wind, King Kong* and *Sleeping Beauty* are just a few of the movies that people lined the streets outside the Capitol Theatre to see. The theater also offered an escape from the everyday factory life that many Flint residents dealt with.

In 1957, the theater was remodeled to fit the times. Much of the ornamentation was removed, the cream walls were repainted battleship gray and an addition was erected to the third story.

In the 1970s, the Capitol Theatre started hosting rock concerts. AC/DC, Black Sabbath, Ray Charles, John Mellencamp and many others played in the ornate theater. This transformation brought the downtown hot spot back to life for a couple of decades. The theater was purchased in 1977 by local grocer George Farah. It has been in the National Register of Historical Places since 1985.

A view of downtown Flint and the Capitol Theatre. *Courtesy of Ari Napolitano.*

As the years moved on, the factories moved out of Flint. Suburban malls and large concert halls were built. The Capitol Theatre was no longer the top venue for entertainment. The once bustling entertainment icon closed its doors in the 1990s. Only a few businesses in the building remained open.

The Farah family worked hard on preserving its grand appearance, but they just could not afford to fully restore the building to its original glory. In 2004, the family received local grant money and did more than $100,000 in repairs on the exterior. But it wasn't enough to bring the old girl back to life.

In 2007 the theater was spruced up for the movie *Semi-Pro* with Will Ferrell, Woody Harrelson and André Benjamin. Scenes were filmed inside the theater and at several locations around Flint. Many of the scenes didn't make the final cut, including a large celebration scene at the Capitol filled with local extras.

Over the years, further renovation attempts started and stalled. In 2015, the Farah family sold the Capitol to the nonprofit Uptown Reinvestment Corporation. Restoration began in 2016.

After sitting mostly dormant for twenty years, the theater was finally fully renovated in a partnership between the Flint Cultural Center Corporation, Whiting Auditorium and the Uptown Reinvestment Corporation. The Whiting now manages the Capitol's programming and marketing.

The $37 million renovations brought the Capitol Theatre back to its original glory. The renovation of the 1,600-seat theater includes restorations of its historic architecture as well as twenty-first-century upgrades. The plain third-story addition was removed, the offices and storefronts were rehabilitated and the theater itself was restored to look like it did in 1928, but with modern upgrades like a digital projector, a new screen for movies and state-of-the-art stage equipment.

The doors of the Capitol reopened in December 2017 to reveal a stunning transformation. From the moment you walk in, you see spectacular attention to detail. The ceiling's ornate medallions were hand-painted, Michelangelo-style. The painters lay on their backs on scaffolding while painting the ceiling. It once again looks like the night sky, complete with twinkling stars and constellations lit by LED lights.

The theater seating was reduced to 1,500 to meet modern building codes, the original marquee and blade sign were replicated by Signs by Crannie with aluminum and LED light bulbs and parts of the old arcade were incorporated into the lobby and first-floor restrooms. An additional elevator was added and the refreshment stand relocated.

Above: The Capitol Theatre with completed renovations. *Courtesy of Ari Napolitano.*

Left: Inside the Capitol Theatre. *Courtesy of Joe Schipani.*

Did the renovation drive the ghosts away or make them come out to play? For years, staff and patrons of the theater have reported seeing ghostly ushers and hearing screams, moans and tapping on the walls inside the auditorium. Some wonder if the spirits are still enjoying concerts long ago seen by human eyes. Ghostly apparitions have been seen on the balcony, on the stage and by the back door. During sound checks for rock concerts in the 1970s, '80s and '90s, band equipment would often randomly stop working, even when the electricity was on. No source for the interruptions was ever discovered.

In the late 1980s and early '90s, the old basement bowling alley space was nicknamed the "Fallout Shelter," and punk rockers would hang out during and after concerts. Many ghost sightings were reported during this time, including a ghostly usher and a workman. Several claims were made of hearing knocks and screams coming from inside the walls, which sparked rumors that someone had been sealed in a wall. There are also reports of disembodied singing echoing through the empty theater and a ghostly glowing girl sitting on the stage.

Is there any history that can tell us who may be haunting the theater? Perhaps one ghost is accounted for. In the 1930s, a man robbed one of the stores across the alley from the theater's back door while a film was playing. The police were called, and gunshots were exchanged. A stray bullet went straight through the back door, killing an employee who had been standing there. The movie was so loud that none of the theatergoers heard the scuffle. And no one heard the employee's anguished screams as he bled to death.

Maybe this man still haunts the theater, hoping someone will finally notice his distress.

8

CARRIAGE TOWN

The Carriage Town area of the city is the heart of Flint. Early Native Americans camped in the area, and Flint's first settler, Jacob Smith, made his home there in 1819.

Factory One on Water Street dates to 1880, when it was built by the Flint Woolen Mills Company. In 1886, William Crapo "Billy" Durant and business partner Josiah Dallas Dort leased the facility for the Flint Road Cart Company, which became the Durant-Dort Carriage Factory.

The Durant-Dort Carriage Company was once the world's largest producer of horse-drawn carriages. In 1908, Billy Durant moved on from horse-drawn carriages to automobiles. He formed the General Motors Corporation in the Durant-Dort Office Building on Water Street.

Over the years, Factory One housed countless other businesses before being abandoned. GM purchased its birthplace in 2013 and renovated the building to showcase the beautiful original architecture. It opened to the public in 2017 as a rental space for events and conferences. Factory One also houses Kettering University's extensive historical and automotive archive.

In the 1980s, around the time Auto World was built, Carriage Town's revitalization started. The Carriage Town name was chosen in 1982 by "civic minded residents of the neighborhood who were organizing for community action against neglect and decay." Much like Flint's moniker, Vehicle City, Carriage Town was inspired by the area's history and connection to carriage manufacturing.

A view of Carriage Town and the Flint River. *Courtesy of Joe Schipani.*

Carriage Town's revitalization has continued for decades. Many of the old homes have been purchased and renovated. In 2009, Gordon Young, former Flint resident and author of *Tear-Down*, published an article in the *New York Times* about Carriage Town: "In a city that is synonymous with faded American industrial and automotive power, Carriage Town's success is both unexpected and inspiring. A persistent group of long-term urban homesteaders—along with newer arrivals eager to live near a downtown showing signs of life—has restored dozens of Victorian-era houses and buildings in the last twenty years. While many Flint neighborhoods feel all but abandoned, in Carriage Town homeownership has increased 10 percent over the last decade, according to Census data."

Flint's historic Carriage Town district's boundaries are Fifth Avenue on the north, North Saginaw Street on the east, the Flint River on the south and Begole Street and Atwood Stadium on the west.

In a place filled with so much history, it is no wonder ghosts linger. David Traxler, the co-owner of the Flint Pantaloon Company, which opened in

Right: The Traxler House in Carriage Town. *Courtesy of Joe Schipani.*

Below: An image of the Paine House from 1907. *Carriage Town Archives.*

The Dunbar House in Carriage Town. *Courtesy of Joe Schipani.*

1896, once lived on Mason Street. Many people have reported seeing a woman in the window near the second-story balcony, even though the house was empty.

Across the street from the Traxler house, in another Mason Street home, people have felt invisible hands trying to push them down the stairs.

Several other historic homes in Carriage Town have similar stories. On West Fourth Avenue is a house built in 1907 for David and Lilla Paine. David worked at the Durant-Dort Carriage Factory for a while before becoming partner at the real estate firm Paine & Darby. David Paine died on June 30, 1918, in Livingston County on his way home from Ann Arbor. Lilla loved her home and did not want to leave. She turned the home into a duplex so she could rent space out, make money and afford to stay in her home. She lived there until 1932, when she had to move in with her sister Edna.

The current resident has experienced many strange things in six years living in the home: footsteps, voices, loud slamming noises, pictures falling off the walls and the feeling of being touched. The house has been repeatedly blessed and smudged, but the strange things continue.

Joseph Dunbar built the Begole Street house in 1899. He and his wife, Mary Ann (Bigler) Dunbar, moved to the home from their previous residence on West Third Avenue. Joseph was one of the most prolific contractors and builders in Flint. He began his carpenter apprenticeship at the age of fifteen. He went into business for himself at the age of seventeen. He came to Flint in 1878 and worked with M.C. Landers, later partnering with P.F. Cleveland to erect St. Michael on Fifth Avenue. They built the dining room and kitchen for the Michigan School for the Deaf. In 1883, Dunbar went into business for himself and at one time had the largest group of men working in the city at one time. His company erected an entire block of stores on First Street, one on Saginaw Street and many residences for prominent members of Flint society.

Joseph and his wife resided in the Begole Street house until their deaths, Mary in 1913 and Joseph in 1914. Joseph passed away in his bedroom. The current resident of the home has a child who will not sleep in that room without the lights on, because she says there is someone there.

Joseph Dunbar built the house on Stone Street for his eldest daughter, Lena. Franklin G. Sutherland and Lena Dunbar Tandy Sutherland married in 1903. Franklin Sutherland was the vice-president of the W.F. Stewart Manufacturing Company. He and Lena resided in the home until their deaths—Franklin in 1938 and Lena in 1951. Several people have reported weird energy in the home and an oppressive feeling by the back stairs.

9

FILLED WITH HISTORY

AVONDALE AND GLENWOOD CEMETERIES

AVONDALE CEMETERY

Located on the edge of downtown Flint nestled between an empty National Guard armory and boarded-up buildings is one of Flint's oldest cemeteries, Avondale. It lies in an area where gentrification has not yet reached and perhaps never will.

Aventine Cemetery is also there, so close to Avondale that they look like one cemetery when you walk around the grounds. Aventine is the burial site of several area Civil War veterans as well as veterans from other eras. It is located on a portion of the grounds of Camp Thomson, a Civil War–era rendezvous and training facility named after Colonel Edward H. Thomson of Flint. The cemetery was abandoned by the City of Flint and left in disrepair. The Brothers of the Gov. Crapo Camp No. 145 decided to "adopt" the cemetery as a project, and they keep it minimally maintained.

It is hard to tell where one cemetery ends and the other begins.

This sad, haphazard cemetery is full of crumbling headstones and toppled monuments that no one cares enough to repair. In recent years, the cemetery has been repeatedly vandalized. The vandals not only damaged physical stones but also destroyed parts of Flint's history and heritage. Many of the stones were over one hundred years old.

"Avondale represents people of all walks of life from Flint, from the mayor to the working person," said David White, president of the Genesee County Historical Society, in an interview with the *Flint Journal*. "It's very unnerving to see the damage because it's so disrespectful to the buried and so costly to repair."

At some point in the summer of 2018, a large tree had split and fallen on top of numerous grave sites. Photos from July show it must have been recent, because it was still full of green leaves that had not completely dried up and crumbled. The tree branches and leaves concealed countless headstones and gravesites. The cemetery had been mowed, but that was the only maintenance that occurred in the sad and lonely city of the dead. Photos from December 2018 show the same tree, dead and leafless, still lying across numerous gravesites. No one had taken care of the problem in the six-month time span.

Modern cemeteries are carefully planned and mapped out. Avondale is a scattered mess. Plots and stones are everywhere, with seemingly no rhyme or reason. Some of this may be due to the old Flint Cemetery residents being disinterred and reburied in Avondale in the 1950s, when the city moved roads and a hotel was built on top of the old cemetery grounds.

Old Flint City Cemetery was established in 1842, when Flint was still a village. By the 1950s, the cemetery was overgrown and no one was taking care of it. In 1952 1,199 residents of the Old Flint City Cemetery were disinterred and reburied at the new Flint City Cemetery on Linden Road and Pasadena Avenue. In 1958, what was thought to be the remaining residents of Old Flint City Cemetery, along with 122 grave markers, were moved to Avondale Cemetery. That area of Avondale is called Pioneer's Row.

Local historians think that many remains were never moved, that only the grave markers found their way to Avondale. This means that many of Flint's early pioneers may remain under Flint parking lots. The historians think that Albert J. Koerts, the man who purchased the Old Flint City Cemetery property, did this to save money. But he was killed in an automobile accident in 1969, taking the truth to *his* grave. Perhaps the restless spirits whose bodies were separated from their headstones wander the grounds trying to find a peaceful resting spot where they can be remembered.

Are secrets and restless spirits the reason something sinister lurks in the shadows of this old cemetery? The Necro Tourist website claims that Avondale is known for orbs and strange noises. Many people claim to have experienced weird things on the grounds. Recently, a couple was exploring Avondale and the outskirts of the abandoned Country Dairy building on Chavez Drive and stumbled across the dead body of a homeless man. That wasn't the first body found outside of Avondale. In 1974, the body of fifteen-year-old Moira Lis was found near the cemetery. Her murder was

An Avondale Cemetery mausoleum. *Courtesy of Ari Napolitano.*

never solved. Crime Stoppers of Flint recently posted her details with a cash reward of up to $2,500 for a tip that leads to an arrest in her case.

Most of the cemetery combines creepiness with the sadness of being forgotten, filled with decrepit grave stones, eerie crypts and mausoleums that have become one with the natural surroundings. But there is one place that really emits a sense of dread. You'll find it in the back of the cemetery when you circle the grounds to make your way out.

An Avondale Cemetery mausoleum. *Courtesy of Ari Napolitano.*

The source of the cemetery's sinister subtext seems to originate from a derelict shed hiding in shadowed darkness in the back of the cemetery. The crumbling building has been mostly taken over by nature and has a huge pile of debris in front of it. Trees and vines had almost swallowed the structure whole. Only one garage door is visible, and it hangs open, darkness reaching out from its depth. Something evil lingers in that old shed.

GLENWOOD CEMETERY

There is a sharp contrast between the somewhat shabby status of Avondale and the well-kept grounds of Glenwood.

Founded in 1857, Glenwood Cemetery is one of Flint's oldest cemeteries. Built along the southern end of the Flint River, in the rolling hills just outside of Flint's center, the cemetery was designed as a romantic garden getaway from city life. It was a place to breathe in fresh air, restore peace and have a family picnic before the creation of city parks.

The Glenwood grounds consist of thirty-three acres of rolling, wooded hills divided into two sections: a western and an eastern park. They are connected by a wooded path, though I would not recommend trying to use it unless you are a skilled hiker. Erosion is destroying many of the hilly pathways, making them almost impossible to walk on, especially when the ground is wet, soggy or icy.

The cemetery's western side contains headstones that are older than those in the eastern portion, although the "grandfathers' corner," as former groundskeeper Peter Lemelin called the tiny section that holds the graves of the cemetery's founders, is on the eastern half.

Glenwood, known as "Flint's Historic Cemetery," was added to the Michigan Register of Historic Places in 1989 and the National Register of Historic Places in 2010. In 2015, Glenwood became a certified arboretum, thanks to its massive oaks, beautiful maples and gnarled catalpa trees.

Strolling through Glenwood, you'll find a historical who's who of the people who made the city of Flint. Even if you don't know Flint history, you'll recognize street, business and building names on the gravestones. Among the stones you'll find Jacob Smith, the founder of Flint, along with lumber barons, Civil War veterans, Michigan governors and pioneers of the carriage and automobile industries. This is just a sample of the names of Glenwood's residents that now grace Flint locations: William S. Ballenger Sr. (Ballenger Highway), Josiah W. Begole (Begole Street), Henry H. Crapo (Crapo Street), J. Dallas Dort (Dort Highway), Williams M. Fenton (the city of Fenton), Charles Stewart Mott (Mott Community College, Mott Children's Health Center, the Mott Foundation), Robert J. Whaley (Whaley House) and James H. Whiting (the Whiting).

"Not many places in a city collect history the way Glenwood has for Flint. A walk around the grounds will transport visitors into all the adventure, triumph, and occasionally, all the heartache of past eras. No chronicle reads quite as eloquently as the graves at Glenwood. "Look out over this cemetery at the names on the headstones," says Peter Lemelin. In "Glenwood Cemetery: A Place of Peace," Jessica Pressley Sinnott writes, "They are the names of the streets we drive on, the parks we play in, and the schools we send our kids to. Glenwood is the home of the city's past, giving to the living a tranquil sanctuary as it gives to the dead a resting place."

Glenwood is peaceful and mysterious. Ornate stones full of imagery make us wonder who these people really were, who loved them, what their lives were like. Headstones full of symbology draw taphophiles. "An obelisk broken in half represents a young woman taken before her time; a stone in the shape

The Mott family mausoleum in Glenwood Cemetery. *Courtesy of Ari Napolitano.*

of a wooden stump marks the final resting place of not only a person but also a line, the last to carry a surname. Many headstones have what appear to be sheets draped over them, representing the thin veil between life and death" (Scott Atkinson, "Lost Orphans").

"Oak leaves indicate strength and longevity, while lilies of the valley symbolize innocence or purity. Two of the saddest symbols are shorn tree limbs and broken columns, the former denoting an absence of lineage, usually due to the loss of a child, while the latter indicates a life cut short" (Jessica Pressley Sinnott, "Glenwood Cemetery: A Place of Peace").

One mysterious set of gravestones even had former Glenwood caretaker Peter Lemelin perplexed. "The three gravestones bear the names Paterson, Pierce, and Hubbard. The men they mark are not related, but all have the same kind of headstone, made from the same kind of stone, and they're in a perfect triangle. Perfect triangle, three exact stones, you think that was an accident? I don't have an answer to it" (Scott Atkinson, "Back to the Bricks).

When you step into Glenwood on a sunny summer day, expect to be welcomed into a shady place, a blissful retreat from the heat of the sun. You may see chipmunks and other furry critters scampering into the bushes as you walk the grounds. On one side of Glenwood is a large mausoleum you can't miss. The elegant tomb sadly attracts vandals regularly. One sunny summer day, it looked as if someone had recently broken into the large mausoleum—or *something* had broken out. In the front of the building, a board lay on the ground in front of an open window. On the side of the building, slats were sticking out from the window in a peculiar manner as if something had torn through them and pushed out from the inside. It was very odd.

Did Glenwood have a zombie outbreak? Perhaps a vampire rising from its burial tomb? Or just Flint teenagers trying to get a peek inside?

A small family crypt lies behind the large mausoleum, quiet and elegant, where a shattered cherub was found lying next to a column on the cement. Such odd things make you pause and wonder. Did this just fall and break, landing here in this position? Or is there a deeper meaning to this shattered visage of innocence?

Glenwood is just as intriguing in winter. Stroll through the older portion of the cemetery and take a trip back in time with Flint historical figures: Mott, Dort, Whiting, Crapo, Smith and Stockton. On a chilly January day, there will probably not be another living soul to disturb you within the cemetery

Glenwood Cemetery's large mausoleum. *Courtesy of Ari Napolitano.*

Glenwood mausoleum window ripped open. *Courtesy of Ari Napolitano.*

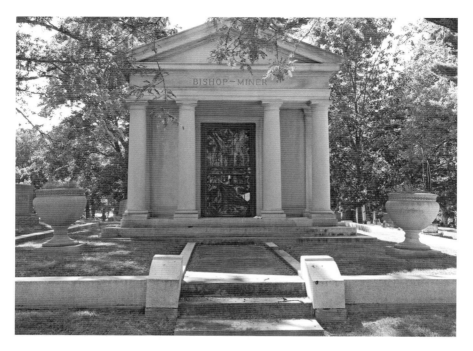

Bishop-Miner family mausoleum, Glenwood Cemetery. *Courtesy of Ari Napolitano.*

gates. It is a stark contrast to the bustling movement outside the gates of Glenwood, where people mill about, walking Flint's streets and waiting on buses while sirens blare in the distance.

Inside the gates, the city sounds are muted and the crunch of dry leaves and the melody of birdsong will fill your ears as you stroll the grounds and imagine how things were in the times when these people were alive.

But even in such a peaceful place, there are stories of hauntings. One passerby claims to have seen a little girl all alone, wearing a pretty dress and riding a scooter, her hair done up in ribbons and curls. The cemetery is not in a good area. Who would let a little girl play outside by herself? Did this passerby catch a glimpse of a playful spirit?

There is another haunting tale tied to Glenwood, the death of Leslie Casteel. In April 1931, Casteel and his girlfriend, Helen Joy Morgan, were having a disagreement and drove to a secluded area in the cemetery to talk. Soon after they parked, shots rang out. Casteel was dead.

Helen Morgan was from a wealthy family, and Leslie Casteel was an illiterate auto mechanic, ten years her senior, who had been married three times and was known to be a serial philanderer. A few months before his death, Casteel had been arrested on suspicion of arson. He was suspected of burning his house down to collect the insurance money. He was painted as the villain, at first.

Helen's story was that he forced her into his car and made her drive to the cemetery. He was angry because she had spoken to the police about him burning down his home the day before and because he thought she was engaged to someone else. When they parked, she was able to get his gun away from him and shoot him dead in self-defense.

Five shots were fired from a .32 caliber revolver. Three passed through his body. A witness claims Morgan then dragged Casteel's body from the car, turned him over to make sure he was dead, then hopped back in the car and drove away.

The police were skeptical of Morgan's version of events. It was eventually uncovered that she was a jealous and possessive girlfriend and that she brought the gun to the meeting. Morgan was convicted of second-degree murder on January 14, 1932. She was sentenced to twenty to twenty-five years in prison.

Could Casteel's ghost be a restless spirit doomed to wander the cemetery forever?

10

SUNSET HILLS AND RIVER REST CEMETERIES

EERILY LIFELIKE STATUES

E stablished in 1926 on the outskirts of Flint's city limits, in the rolling hills of what use to be Flint's countryside, is Sunset Hills and River Rest Cemeteries. The beautifully wooded grounds offered eace and escape from the hustle and bustle of a booming city.

Sunset Hills is a beautiful cemetery full of lush lawns, shady trees, classy mausoleums and a maze of roads winding between gravestones and monuments. In the spring, thousands of white daffodils surround the cemetery's entrances. The interior landscape is filled with flower gardens that add color to the picturesque forest backdrop. A garden with stone pillars and wisteria vines is a picturesque spot for a memorial service or the scattering of cremation ashes.

But this beautiful cemetery is home to one of the most well-known urban legends and ghost stories in the Flint area, thanks to its lifelike statues.

Currently, the cemetery has eight statues.

Check It Out by Jerry Boyle. The sculpture, of a young girl carrying an armload of books, is no longer in the cemetery. It is on permanent loan to the Flint Public Library.

Jesus Christ. A Carrara marble sculpture purchased in Italy that depicts Christ with open arms.

The Generation Bridge by J. Seward Johnson, which showcases a grandfather seated on a bench talking with his granddaughter.

The Gardener by J. Seward Johnson. This very realistic guy is out night and day, rain or shine, planting from a bronze flat of flowers.

The Generation Bridge by J. Seward Johnson. *Courtesy of Ari Napolitano.*

The Gardener by J. Seward Johnson. *Courtesy of Ari Napolitano.*

Candice and the Flower Girls by Gary Price. *Courtesy of Ari Napolitano.*

Candice and the Flower Girls by Gary Price. Two separate sculptures depict Candice looking as if she is watering the flowers that the younger girls are picking.

Give Me a Kiss by Derek Wernher showcases a man and a woman walking together with a young boy on the man's shoulders.

The Provider by Derek Wernher is a lifelike statue of Albert Koegel filling a bird feeder.

The Flag Raiser by Derek Wernher features former grounds supervisor Charles Smith raising the American flag. He worked at the cemetery for over thirty-nine years.

Crack the Whip by J. Seward Johnson. Eight children play a game of Crack the Whip.

Give Me a Kiss by Derek Wernher. *Courtesy of Ari Napolitano.*

The Flag Raiser by Derek Wernher.
Courtesy of Ari Napolitano.

When you visit Sunset Hills, you might expect to find a creepy land of the dead, thanks to the stories that have circulated for decades. Some find the life-size bronze statues terrifying. If you are not expecting them, they can really startle you, as several are extremely lifelike. Especially *The Gardener*. A sideways glance out of the corner of your eye…yeah, he looks real. The cemetery often places real plants in his tray of gardening supplies during the warmer months.

At night, the statues can seem sinister. Imagine creeping through the darkness of the cemetery, then stumbling upon a figure standing in the shadows, not moving. Just watching you…

The most popular statue and the first to be added to the cemetery was *Crack the Whip*. It cost a whopping $85,000 in 1983 and was made by J. Seward Johnson Jr. Because of this statue, many people refer to the cemetery simply as "Crack the Whip." Supposedly, this statue was dedicated in 1983 by an anonymous Flint resident who had family buried in the cemetery. Is there more of a backstory to this sculpture?

Old urban legends abound. One tale claims that children from the area were playing Crack the Whip when the little girl at the end of the "whip" lost her grip and was thrown into oncoming traffic. She was tragically hit by a car and died. Part of this legend also claims that the statue was donated by the girl's grandfather in honor of her memory. This legend is unsubstantiated.

In fact, the Flint radio station Banana 101.5 did some research and found that neither version of the statue's origin story is true. Banana's research discovered that the original *Crack the Whip* statue was created in 1980. Sunset Hills thought it would be a nice addition to the cemetery and purchased a recasting in 1983. The girl at the end of the whip was based on J. Seward Johnson Jr.'s younger sister, who is still alive.

Crack the Whip features an Asian girl, two African American kids, a Native American and four white kids. The Asian girl lost her sandal. It lies in the grass nearby. And that sandal is the centerpiece of the terrifying legends.

Crack the Whip by J. Seward Johnson. *Courtesy of Ari Napolitano.*

Crack the Whip and *Sandal. Courtesy of Ari Napolitano.*

The Sandal, featured in all the ghost stories and urban legends. *Courtesy of Ari Napolitano.*

In addition to the rumors that you can hear the sounds of children playing, giggling and crying near the statue, there are several versions of the urban legend that have floated around over the years. One legend says if your foot fits in the shoe, something terrible will happen to you. Another, that if your foot fits in the shoe, you will die soon. Another claims that the eight child statues have been cursed and that the Asian girl who lost her shoe holds the power of the curse.

Another legend claims that if you visit the statue at midnight and your foot fits in the shoe, the statues will come to life. If you've seen the statues at night, you can easily imagine them coming to life. In fact, they almost seem to be alive in daylight. The movement captured in the *Crack the Whip* sculpture makes it easy to believe the kids are in motion. Imagine seeing them in the dark of night under the moonlight.

The legend of the Crack the Whip has been around as long as the statue. Teenagers in the 1990s dared one another to sneak into the cemetery at night and try on the shoe. Kids also liked to wander around the ruins of the Walter Winchester Memorial Hospital that was next to Sunset Hills. Teens would party there all the time. Rumors swirled that devil worship and occult sacrifices took place at the site. By the 1990s, the hospital was no more than an empty shell covered in graffiti and littered with trash. But it wasn't the trash or the graffiti that was the problem. It was the gut-wrenching, hair-standing-on-end feeling of horror that sent many running from the site. No one knows what resided in those ruins, but if you were smart, you steered clear of them.

Thankfully, that creepy shell of a building was torn down years ago, and all that remains is empty land.

Inside Sunset Hills, the statues continue to be a draw. They are beautiful works of art. But their beauty doesn't overpower superstition. The stories and legends continue to fascinate and terrify Flint locals to this day.

Would you dare to try on the shoe?

Crack the Whip isn't the only haunt in Sunset Hills. Near the *Crack the Whip* statue is a bench located in a shady spot on a slight hill. It is such an inviting spot to relax in the shade. The accompanying photo was taken of that bench. No one noticed the startling human-shaped blur sitting on the bench until the photo was uploaded to a computer.

Do you see it? Is it a ghost? *Courtesy of Roxanne Rhoads.*

Skeptics, of course, claim it to be lens flare. Believers swear it is a ghost. One person even blended the metaphysical with science to offer an explanation. "The apparition's energy bent the light and caused the light flare to take place. It's like thermal imaging recorders; the spirit shows up because its effect on the temperature of the environment bends and causes it to have a shape in the camera because its energy field creates the shape." Sounds legit.

Don't you think it is interesting that this "haunting" blur appears near the Crack the Whip statue, the one with all the legends, rumors and ghost stories attached to it?

Perhaps there is something to all the ghost stories after all.

11

Oak Grove Sanitarium, the Flint Cultural Center and Central High School

Oak Grove Sanitarium

In 1891, the Oak Grove Sanitarium was established as an upscale hospital for the treatment of mental disorders and addictions. The sanitarium resembled a castle more than a stark institution. It was designed to "provide a home-like setting for people of refined tastes, who were accustomed to the luxuries and conveniences of life." The sixty-five-acre property had nine buildings that featured dining halls, patient rooms and administration, entertainment and treatment centers including artesian wells. Patients could "avail themselves of the superior advantages it offered, including hydrotherapeutic and electric treatment for the relief of nervous prostration." Many nurses were highly skilled in massage and the latest treatment methods of the time.

Oak Grove was luxurious. Even the food was "the very best quality, delicately cooked and promptly served." Milk was furnished by a private herd of hand-selected cows. The Noyse Amusement Building contained a bowling alley, gymnasium, billiards room, Turkish baths and hydrotherapy rooms.

Yet underneath all the shining luxury, darkness lurked, as it often does in institutions. Oak Grove served as a place where the wealthy could dispose of problematic family members—those who actually had mental issues or addictions and those who were simply troublesome. Oak Grove was nothing more than a gilded cage, and the only escape was death. Several patients

Oak Grove Sanitarium, Flint, Mich.

Oak Grove Sanitarium looked more like a castle than a hospital. *Courtesy of Daniel Conner.*

died at the facility, including William Wells and Peter H. Struthers. There are also a few suicides on record.

During its twenty-nine years of operation, Oak Grove received patients from every state in the union and Canada. In 1920, the Flint Board of Education purchased Oak Grove.

The Flint Cultural Center and the now closed Flint Central High School are located on the grounds of the old Oak Grove Sanitarium.

FLINT CENTRAL HIGH SCHOOL

Flint Central's imposing size and gorgeous architecture loom large and empty between the grounds of the cultural center and Mott Community College.

Abandoned and left to vandals, it has quickly fallen into disrepair and is a favorite of urban-exploration photographers, some of whom have reported hearing strange sounds, seeing shadow people and having ghostly encounters during their artistic endeavors to get great photos of this once-beautiful building.

Central High School entrance covered in graffiti. *Courtesy of Ari Napolitano.*

Central High School. *Courtesy of Ari Napolitano.*

One ghost-hunting couple shared several grainy photos on the "Haunted Flint" Facebook page that were taken in the ruins of Flint Central High School and the tunnels beneath. The images feature orbs, shadowy figures and full-blown apparitions. Whether they are real or edited is not known, but they sure are creepy.

Rumors of the eerie tunnels underneath Central abound and can be traced back to Oak Grove. It is said that tunnels connected some of the nine buildings of the sanitarium and were later used to connect the buildings that made up Flint Central High School and Whittier Junior High School.

One original building from Oak Grove remains: the old stable.

Many urban explorers have tried to find all the tunnels, but only one is documented as being found by explorers. It leads into Central High School.

THE FLINT CULTURAL CENTER

In 1955, Flint's centennial year, a plan was created for the city's cultural development. The land was provided by Charles Stewart Mott, a GM director and former Flint mayor. Mott offered up part of the acreage of his Applewood Estate. The Flint Board of Education provided land from the Oak Grove campus.

Applewood still sits at the edge of the cultural center. The inside of the estate is a museum frozen in time; things remain exactly as Mott left them. The garden is open for the public to enjoy May through October, and many community events are held on the grounds. Applewood is controlled by the Ruth Mott Foundation. Applewood Estate is a Michigan Historic Landmark and is listed in the National Register of Historic Places.

In 1958, Robert T. Longway Planetarium, the Flint Institute of Arts, the Flint Public Library, the F.A. Bower Theatre and the Enos A. & Sarah DeWaters Art Center opened on the cultural center campus. Next came the Flint Institute of Music, and in 1966, the Alfred P. Sloan Museum was built. Construction was completed on the two-thousand-seat James H. Whiting Auditorium in 1966. The first performance at the theater occurred in October 1967. In 1999, the theater was renovated and became known simply as "The Whiting."

Over the years, many renovations, remodels and name changes have occurred at the cultural center. As of this writing, a school is being built on the cultural center campus to provide community children with quality education with a heavy emphasis on the arts.

Two of the cultural center buildings have reported ghostly activity.

SLOAN MUSEUM

Museums full of antiquities and historical artifacts are a common place for ghost sightings. Several employees at Flint's Sloan Museum have had spooky encounters they can't explain.

One night, when an employee, Joshua, was ready to close for the night, he made the closing announcement then walked the museum to let everyone know they would be closing in thirty minutes. While making the rounds, he encountered two older couples and a young woman with her two children. He had to sidestep one of the children so the child didn't bump into him.

After walking the square of the museum, he arrived back at the front desk. His coworker Jen went into the back to clean up. While Joshua was at the desk, the two older couples exited the museum. Jen came back to the front and told Joshua the woman and her children were still playing in the children's area.

Joshua made a final closing announcement then went to the back to let them know it was time to go. They were not there. He assumed they had made their way out while he was walking to the back. Arriving at the front again, he asked Jen if they had exited. She said they had not. There are no other exits. Joshua walked around one more time, then checked all the offices, restrooms and the courtyard. No one. He even asked Jen's mom, who was waiting out front, if she had seen anyone exit. Her response was that she had seen two older couples. He went back and checked sales records for the day. At no point had they rung up ticket sales for an adult and two children.

Another story from Joshua happened one night when Sloan Museum rented space to Kettering for a special event. A professor mentioned to him and his coworker Greg that it was really cool that they had costumed staff for the event and mentioned seeing a woman in old-fashioned clothing. Joshua and Greg looked at each other then told the professor that as a nonprofit, Sloan had no budget for costumed actors. The professor laughed then realized they were serious. They all went searching for the woman but never found her.

THE WHITING

Employees of The Whiting have been reporting ghostly sightings for decades: shadowy figures, disembodied voices and unexplained footsteps. Some feel a presence in the auditorium. Many people have heard phantom footsteps in empty corridors and on the lower balcony. But most of the sightings come from the stage area. One night, a cleaning person saw a man wearing workman's clothes on the stage who simply disappeared.

Joshua, who worked both at Sloan and The Whiting, had several encounters at The Whiting. He often heard voices coming from the stage. One night, he heard two men talking upstairs, but he and his coworker Wendi were the only ones in the building.

In November 2009, Mid-Michigan Paranormal Investigators visited The Whiting with their gear to see if they could find evidence of lurking spirits. They recorded many EMF fluctuations, caught unexplained voices on their recording devices and music notes of no known origin. One member of the team even claimed to see a shadowy figure of a man in work clothes and work boots.

There have been two deaths in the theater: a guest passed away during the production of *Oklahoma!*, and a construction worker stumbled while on a scaffold and fell to his death on the stage.

12

SPENCER HOUSE OF MORTUARY

Old mortuaries are always rumored to be haunted. They've held so many dead bodies that it's not a big leap to think a few spirits might linger long after their bodies were transported elsewhere.

Built in 1910, the Spencer House has had many incarnations. For many years, the multifamily duplex housed factory workers and businessmen. In the 1930s, it was the home of Fred Dibble and his family. Fred is the grandson of Clark Dibble, who founded the town Dibbleville in 1834, a location known today as the city of Fenton.

The home was purchased by Dr. Merrill Spencer and his wife, Edith, in 1955. The Spencers converted the home into the Spencer House of Mortuary for African Americans. Dr. and Mrs. Spencer were both predominant leaders in the NAACP and the civil rights movement. Edith Spencer was also an activist with the League of Women Voters who worked to help African American women receive voting education.

During its more than forty years, the home was a mortuary. It not only provided a place for people to say goodbye to loved ones but also doubled as a meeting place for the NAACP and the civil rights movement in Flint.

In the 1950s, Dr. Spencer purchased cemetery plots in the whites-only cemetery, Flint Memorial Park. When his mother died in 1964, the cemetery would not allow him to bury her there. He took the case all the way to the Michigan Court of Appeals and finally won the right to have his mother's body moved and buried at Flint Memorial Park in 1966. This court case changed the segregation laws in Michigan cemeteries.

Edith Spencer took part in the family business by becoming one of the first African American women to become a mortician in Flint. She graduated with honors from the Wayne State School of Mortuary Science. She already had a business degree. In addition to her active role in the family business and her involvement in the civil rights movement, Edith Spencer also held a full-time position at the Flint Public Library. She retired from the library in 1987 after more than thirty years of service.

The Spencers operated the mortuary for over forty years before retiring and closing the business in 1997. Since then, the home has been boarded up, left to decay and often used as a gathering place for the customers of the neighboring liquor store.

Mrs. Spencer donated Spencer House of Mortuary to the Historic Carriage Town Neighborhood Association.

The Flint Public Art Project turned the mortuary into a center for the arts in 2012.

Former funeral homes almost always have rumors about remains being left behind after the business closes its doors. In 99 percent of the cases, there is no truth to the rumors. However, there was one funeral home in Flint where human remains were discovered long after the business had shut down, but it was not Spencer House of Mortuary. In 2006, human ashes were found in

Spencer House before it was torn down. *Courtesy of Joe Schipani.*

the shuttered Collins Memorial Funeral Home on Clio Road. In 2017, the State of Michigan revoked the mortuary license of Swanson Funeral Home in Flint after discovering stacks of unrefrigerated bodies and numerous other violations. It also found three hundred sets of unclaimed cremains, which were eventually laid to rest at New Calvary Catholic Cemetery.

The realtor who handled Spencer House said there were several caskets and an old embalming room left behind but no cremains, bodies or body parts.

Other rumors that swirl about Spencer House include shadowy figures that linger in the windows and screams and cries that can be heard when you walk by the house at night.

On May 14, 2016, the Haunt Investigators of Michigan did a paranormal investigation at Spencer House. It was a dreary, cold and rainy night when Joe had the chance to take part in their investigation. During the investigation, they encountered four spirits, one who gave a name, George Kepler.

The next day, Joe researched George Kepler. He found two that lived in Flint in the 1930s. One of them lived three blocks over on Sixth Avenue. Factory workers rented and moved from house to house quite often. George could have possibly lived in one of the two rental units of the house at some point, but did he die there, too?

The old mortuary was demolished in November 2018. Residents of the neighboring art house started hearing strange noises after the demolition. One night, they were awakened by the sounds of moaning and screaming coming from the property. But when they tried to find the source, no explanation was found.

Were lost spirits left behind after their funerals? Did something sinister happen on the grounds of the mortuary that has caused spirits to hang around, even though the house is gone?

13

THE FLINT TAVERN HOTEL

Built in 1927, this six-story, low-rise hotel was built to catch the overflow of the much larger Durant Hotel. The Flint Tavern's brick exterior, designed by Charles N. Agree, lined the corner of Detroit Street and Third Avenue.

The hotel was designed in the same style as its larger rival, with a grand lobby, restaurant, the Tavern Pharmacy and a couple of small retail stores on its first floor. The tavern offered two hundred nicely decorated rooms within walking distance of the downtown shopping area. The hotel thrived until the 1950s.

In 1958, the Flint Tavern Hotel closed its doors. After much-needed remodeling, the hotel reopened the following year as the Marion Hall for the Elderly. The Flint Tavern was the perfect location, close to all amenities, and it offered a safe place for the elderly of Flint to live. Many elderly residents passed away in the building. The building operated as Marion Hall for several decades until the business moved to the suburbs in the 1980s.

The building didn't stay empty for long. It quickly changed hands to Odyssey House and reopened as a drug rehabilitation house for addicts. With Flint's economy crumbling, drug use and crime were spinning out of control. The once small Odyssey House could no longer function in its small quarters, so when the building became available, they jumped at the chance to move to a much larger facility. The Odyssey House has operated there ever since.

Mural on the side of the old Flint Tavern Hotel. *Courtesy of Roxanne Rhoads.*

Flint Tavern Hotel, now the Odyssey House. *Courtesy of Joe Schipani.*

On quiet mornings at the old Tavern Hotel, some have heard screams on the ground floor by the elevator shaft. Others have claimed to see the shadow of a man entering and leaving the elevator on the fifth floor. The man is thought to be Theodore Schroeder.

In 1928, shortly after the hotel opened, an elevator was installed for the luxury of its guests. On June 30, Theodore Schroeder was sent to the Flint Tavern Hotel to make final adjustments to the elevator in the new hotel. Schroeder stood on a girder between the two shafts; he stepped back and fell five floors to his death. Schroeder's body broke through the safety boards on two different levels before hitting the ground. His skull was busted open. The forty-nine-year-old man died instantly.

On the sixth floor, the spirit of a little girl has been known to join living children for playtime. Who she might be or where she came from is unknown.

14

THE DRYDEN BUILDING

The Dryden Building was erected in 1902 by W.A. Paterson, a carriage maker and major developer of downtown Flint. It stands at the corner of Saginaw and Second Streets.

According to *Flint Journal* archives, the building is named after Paterson's wife, Mary Dryden. In 1921, the building was passed down to Paterson's son William after his death.

A major fire took a toll on the building in 1926, resulting in William rebuilding the structure. The Dryden Building was completely renovated the following year, adding a mezzanine floor and a sixth floor that is unseen from the outside.

In the 1940s, Flint's downtown area had become a retail hot spot. The Dryden Building, with its style and charm, had no problem drawing in high-profile stores like JC Penny, Hill's Bros. and Rosenthal. For decades, the Dryden Building thrived as a retail destination. In the 1970s, stores started to move to the suburbs with the rise of large shopping malls.

Recently, Phil Hagerman, CEO of Diplomat Pharmacy, purchased the building. Extensive renovations turned the Dryden Building into a place for companies and businesses to grow. It is now full of local retail stores and pop-up shops, which are smaller second locations for businesses that have locations elsewhere. Some of the current stores include Julie Abbott Art, Red Fox Outfitters, Bedrock, the Machine Shop and Detroit Muscle.

Several ghost stories have been told about the Dryden Building.

One dark night, an employee was working late in one of the Dryden Building's offices. She thought she was all alone. Then she heard footsteps on the stairs behind her. Closer and closer the footsteps came, echoing loudly through the empty building. As the footsteps got closer, she turned around, but no one was there. The footsteps stopped.

The third floor is known to be full of ghostly activity. Many people have caught sight of a mysterious man pacing and have heard the sounds of people going up and down the stairs when no one is there.

Some have seen a man walking down the hall. A couple of people tried to approach the man, but he disappeared when they got close. One person claimed it was W.A. Paterson, having recognized him from an old photo.

The restroom on the third floor is another ghostly hot spot. Many have claimed that the bathroom has an oppressive feeling. It is so bad that some people will leave the room and find a restroom on another floor.

Did Mr. Paterson love the building so much he never left? Is he protecting his masterpiece from the harm of the new world?

15

THE CORNWALL BUILDING

The Cornwall Building is located at 624 South Grand Traverse. Over the years, it has been home to many people and businesses.

Construction began on the house in the early 1870s by Royal Ripley, who lived on the premises from 1874 to 1881. In 1881, Er Milner purchased the home and completed construction in 1883. The Milner family moved into this beautiful Italianate home designed by Elijah Meyer, the same architect who designed Michigan's capitol building in Lansing.

Er Milner was one of Michigan's pioneers in lumbering. The Milners lived in the home with their two daughters, Winnie and Jennie. The eldest, Jennie, was born on December 21, 1863. On November 27, 1895, Jennie married John Cornwall in the family home. The wedding was a spectacular event attended by family and close friends.

The house was decorated with a mixture of pink and white roses and chrysanthemums, with an archway of flowers in front of the bay window, where the ceremony took place. After the ceremony, the guests were invited to stay for refreshments and cake in the dining room and library, where the Millikins' orchestra played. The guests were some of Flint's most elite citizens, like the Beechers, Durants, Dorts and Motts.

The couple enjoyed a honeymoon in Saginaw then returned to the home of the bride's father, which had been deeded to Jennie as a wedding gift.

John Cornwall was a bookkeeper at the Durant-Dort Carriage Company at the time of their marriage but later became president of the Flint Lumber Company while Jennie took care of her father. On June 12, 1898, Er Milner passed away.

The Wright Building, aka the Cornwall House. *Courtesy of Ari Napolitano.*

John Cornwall arrived in Flint at the age of sixteen from Bristol, England, with his stepmother and sister Clara. He and Clara purchased the Flint Specialty Company in May 1901. With the help of his sister and his skills as a businessman, he turned the company into the largest manufacturer of whip sockets for buggies, carriages and sleighs.

By 1910, the company was producing over a million sockets a year. In the fall of 1920, John became ill with Bright's disease. He left his duties at the company but remained president of the Flint Lumber Company until May 1921, when he lost his battle and passed away in the home on Grand Traverse Street. He was survived by his wife, stepmother and sister.

Jennie Cornwall continued to live in the family home with her maid until her death during World War II in November 1943. The couple never had any children. Rumor has it that Jennie never wanted children, that she detested them so much that they were not even allowed in the home. Children of visitors had to remain in the vestibule when they visited. John's niece Geraldine Chapel was not allowed in the home until after she turned sixteen, and that was only to help with household chores like the ironing.

The Milner family and the Cornwall family now rest in Glenwood Cemetery. When Jennie passed away, she deeded the building to the City of Flint to create a women's health center. Ironically, it was turned into the Cornwall Nursery, a daycare for the children of women who went to work in the factories during the war effort. That had to aggravate Jennie's spirit.

The nursery closed in 1948 and sat empty, becoming a magnet for looters and vandals until 1954, when attorneys John Damm and Arthur Weiss purchased the building and turned it into offices.

In 1974, attorney John M. Wright purchased the building and spent years restoring the seventeen-room structure to its original beauty, paying special attention to the parquet floors, hand-painted fireplaces and ornate woodwork.

There are many tales of shadowy figures, unexplained music and people in the windows, especially eerie when the office building sits empty at night. Many think Jennie never left her lifelong home and that she is the figure often spotted looking out the windows. Walk along Third Street at night and look up at the third-floor window. You might see a ghostly family playing together.

A sideview of the Cornwall House. *Courtesy of Ari Napolitano.*

Carriage house to the Cornwall Building. *Courtesy of Joe Schipani.*

Peer into the windows along the first floor and you may see two women dressed in early twentieth-century attire—one reading while the other is tidying up the place. These ladies are believed to be Jennie and her maid Lillian Bingham. You may also hear the faraway notes of old-fashioned music from John Cornwall's extensive music collection.

Glance over to the old carriage building out back and you may see the shadowy figure of a man walking into the red barn. Some think the man is John Cornwall, who continues to watch over the building. Others claim it is Er Milner readying his carriage for a ride into town.

16

THE CATSMAN HOUSE

The Catsman House was built on the site of a Native American trading post, where it was said that good fortune was spread with every sale. After the land was purchased from the Native Americans, the lot was then home to a couple of small shack-style houses. The small houses were used by fur traders as hunting cabins. At the turn of the twentieth century, the land was developed as an upscale neighborhood for Flint's Jewish community.

In 1919, the owner of Catsman Coal Company, Philip Catsman, built the house that currently stands on the property. The Catsman family lived in the house for almost two decades but was caught up in scandal after scandal into the 1980s.

Their son, Samuel Catsman, was indicted in 1962 for defrauding the city by obtaining money under false pretenses when the city was looking for a new water source. The plans were laid for the city to build a pipeline from Lake Huron to Flint. The indictment caused so much negative attention that the city decided to buy its water from Detroit (which later led to the twenty-first-century water scandal that Flint is known for).

After the Catsman family moved out, the house was sold a couple times, once to an eye doctor, who used the home as an office. The home was then sold to Mr. and Mrs. Hayes in 1949. They lived in the house until their deaths.

Mrs. Hayes outlived her husband by several decades. She was the first female principal of Beecher School. After her husband's passing, Mrs. Hayes

The Catsman House. *Courtesy of Joe Schipani.*

used the large house to her advantage and allowed teachers to board there at a low rate. Throughout the years, many teachers were able to get jobs due to the low cost of living with Mrs. Hayes. She also took in her brother as a border after he returned from crime-ridden Chicago. Rumors swirled that he was a member of the Purple Gang. He had trouble with the law and was placed on probation. Mrs. Hayes allowed him to live with her during his time on probation.

In 1979, Mrs. Hayes died of old age in the front room of the home she loved so much.

The current owner, Pam, was drawn to the house for years. After Mrs. Hayes passed away, Pam jumped at the chance to purchase it when it went on the market in 1980. Pam has owned the home ever since and plans to live there for the rest of her life.

Many strange things have happened at the Catsman house. A medium once told the owner that a Native American, known as the Keeper, had a trading post on the site where the house sits today, and he opened a portal to another world.

In the basement, a man named Hank seems to have taken residence in the tool room. Hank and the owner seem to have an understanding. She puts a small holiday display up for him to enjoy every holiday season and always asks for his permission before taking any tools out of the room. Hank seems to be ok with men coming into the tool room, but he is not ok with women, except the owner of the home. He has locked a few women in the tool room. The owner claims that if Hank likes you, he can be a big help. Whenever she plans on working on a project, he will pull the tools she needs and place them on the workbench. But don't leave your stuff in the tool room. If he doesn't like you, he will throw it out of the room.

On the main floor of the house, the presence of former homeowner Mr. Hayes has made many appearances. He is often seen in the dining room tipping his hat. His presence can often be felt by a touch on the shoulder. While having dinner at the home, Joe was sitting in a chair where Mr. Hayes often appears. Toward the end of dinner, Joe felt a cold hand placed on his shoulder.

In the entryway of the home, a spirit that goes by the name of Jimmy can be found. For the most part, he hangs out in the coat closet, but on occasion, he will open and close doors. This happens frequently enough that the owner has put bells on the front door to keep her from running to the front door and checking to see if someone has come into her house.

The second floor of the home has many haunting tales. While the homeowner was away on vacation, her handyman was redoing the bathroom. He was working on the plumbing when he heard the front door open and close, followed by footsteps coming up the stairs. He waited to see who was coming, thinking it may have been someone else who lived in the house or kept an office there. After a few minutes, when no one appeared, he got up to look. No one was there. This happened to him several times during the bathroom renovation.

Ethel Hayes passed away in the front room, which is now the owner's office. Ethel can be seen in that room on occasion, but she mostly appears on the second floor. One of the owner's friends, who rents a room as office space, heard Ethel Hayes ask her what she was working on. Ethel then proceeded to give her advice.

Ethel Hayes is also great with children. A friend of the owner, who used to live in the home, had her five-year-old granddaughter stay the night. The child said that there was a lady who tucked her in and read to her at night. When asked how she felt about the woman, the child responded that the lady was her friend, but that she was afraid of her.

Other children who have stayed in the home have made the same claim.

In a different second-floor bedroom, the presence of another spirit lives in the large walk-in closet. He has been known to push people out of the closet if they stay in it too long. Joe was able to experience this in my first visit to the home. He stood in the closet for a few minutes then started to feel pressure on the side of his head. It felt like the palm of a hand pushing him out. When he left the closet, a cold spot the size and shape of a hand could be felt on his head.

The third floor is home to three elderly women who are picky about how the space is cleaned. One time, while the owner's partner was cleaning, she heard a voice tell her, "You're not doing that right" and "Get out of my room, you don't know how to clean."

The owner claims that a new spirit recently took up residence on the third floor—a young boy. The three old ladies seem to have taken him in. He likes to get into things. The third floor is the owners' craft space. One time, they found a bag of feathers scattered around the room. They picked them up, put them away and went on to do their crafting. They took a break and went downstairs for a while. When they came back, the feathers were scattered around the room again.

Although there are many spirits in the home, the house has a way of welcoming the guests it likes. Many guests have claimed that the house hugs them as they enter. If you stay long enough, you just might hear them throw a party in your honor.

17

BUICK CITY

I n 1903, David Dunbar Buick founded the Buick Motor Company. The following year, William Durant invested in Buick's company.

Buick produced an automobile known as the Model B in 1904. Thirty-seven were manufactured that year. By 1906, David D. Buick had lost control of the company and sold his shares. In 1908, Billy Durant made Buick the cornerstone of General Motors. In 1923, Buick built its 1,000,000th vehicle. The Buick brand played a key role in General Motors' rise to being the world's largest automaker.

Durant raised hundreds of thousands of dollars to build a huge Buick industrial complex on Flint's north side. Buick's first building off Hamilton Avenue opened in 1908. In 1984, GM brought together multiple factories to form the massive complex named Buick City. It became one of the largest automotive manufacturing facilities in the world. The sprawling 364-acre site ran from Pierson Road to Harriet Street on the south end.

Work conditions in the factories were extremely dangerous for factory workers before the Flint Sit-Down Strike. For forty-four days—from December 30, 1936, to February 11, 1937—the workers fought the GM Corporation in a struggle centered in Flint. GM employed every tactic its strength and cunning could devise, while the workers met attack with counterattack, took the offensive and finally emerged with a decisive victory.

The Flint Sit-Down Strike is considered one of the biggest economic events of the twentieth century for blue-collar workers. "It gave us within the auto industry a voice against management without the fear of

Photo of the Buick factory. *From the book* History of Genesee County, Michigan.

repercussions or losing our jobs," said Art Reyes, former UAW 599 president, in an interview with MLive.com. "It gave us respect in the workplace."

Before the union improved working conditions, hundreds of people died in the factories from heat stroke, machine failure and manufacturing accidents.

By the late 1980s, Buick sales were declining rapidly. In 1997, it was announced that Buick City would close. The final vehicle to roll off the assembly on June 29, 1999, was a Buick LeSabre.

For years, the site sat abandoned and full of toxic levels of waste. In late summer 2018, the Lear Corporation opened a new manufacturing site on thirty-three acres of the old Buick City complex.

Over the years, many tales have been told of ghost sightings and hauntings on the Buick City property. A while back, a friend of Joe's told him a story that she had heard in the 1960s about people seeing an unidentified man walking around the train tracks in Buick City. When people would go to confront the man, he would vanish before they could reach him.

Stories from neighbors who live next to the abandoned site say tortured screams can be heard in the middle of the night. Others have claimed to see things that look like shooting stars moving around the vast wasteland. Some people have heard the sounds of children playing by the train tracks.

Could the screams and lights be the souls of the many who died from heat stroke working there on hot summer days, or are they some of those who were fatally injured working in the plant? Buccio Ambrea died when he was hit on the head with an automatic hammer. Tony Hallock was fatally burned when the boiler exploded. Joe Schaster was killed when he was hit by a crane, and Joseph Crow was fatally injured by a saw. James Caldwil and James Johnston were both killed in a steam explosion in the Buick heating tunnel.

Could the man who walks the tracks be Henry Master, who was found dead beside the tracks in 1921? Or maybe it is Joseph Bolient, who died after being struck in the head by another employee while he was working.

Could the child be Joe Bujarski, who was killed in 1914 while playing on the test tracks? Maybe the sounds of children come from one of the many other children who played on the grounds while their fathers worked in the factory.

Any of the strange sightings on the grounds could be someone listed here or one of the many others whose life was cut short on the massive grounds of Buick City.

Perhaps the stories are just made up tales by bored factory workers or superstitious neighbors. You be the judge.

18

THE FLINT RIVER

The Flint River has made the news a lot in the past several years, thanks to the Flint Water Crisis. But long before that, it has been a source of both prosperity and strife in the Flint area. Many times, the banks of the river have overflowed, causing flooding. But a few such instances are considered to be historic floods.

In February 1938, the ice melted and the rains came, creating horrible flood conditions that saw the river rise two inches per hour.

In early September 1985, storms came in hard and fast, drowning Flint in floodwaters. Around four hundred families were left with split, cracked or collapsed walls, and at least ten homes had roofs caved in from water pressure and wind. Hundreds of residents lost furniture, family heirlooms, furnaces and hot-water heaters when basements filled with water.

In less than eight hours, 7.45 inches of rain fell. Violent storms ripped through the Flint area, causing power outages, mudslides and flooding. Many residents were evacuated from their homes, schools were closed and stores ran out of supplies.

The Flint River crested at a record-breaking seventeen feet. Dozens of streets were flooded, and cars were submerged, including Mount Morris's main police car, an image that made the front page of the *Detroit Free Press*. Patrolman Carlton had been transporting a drunk driver to the Genesee County Jail when the car stalled in the water. While he waited for a wrecker, the floodwaters kept rising until just the light bubble on the top of the car was visible. Poor Officer Carlton's main worry was, "How was I going to tell the chief that I lost the car?"

River View. Flint. Mich.

Postcard of the Flint River. *Author Collection.*

Yet the flood of 1947 is considered to be only one of Flint's worst natural disasters, second only to the tornado of 1953. Allison Rosbury, in "Swept Away: The Flood of 1947," writes, "From April 4–11 1947, a combination of melting snow, moderate-to-intense spring thunderstorms, and increased runoff resulted in downtown Flint's Saginaw Street being submerged under chilly spring waters."

Residents watched cars and buses float down the flooded roadways along with furniture, washing machines and refrigerators. Many of the downtown businesses were forced to relocate after the flood because the damage to their buildings was too extensive. Damages to public and private buildings were estimated at $10 million, according to *Flint Journal* files. At the peak of the flood, the Flint River reached 5.35 feet above flood stage, the worst recorded flood in city history.

A little over seventy-eight miles long, the Flint River flows through three counties: Genesee, Lapeer and Saginaw. The river forms in Lapeer County near Columbiaville, where the river's north and south branch come together. The water volume is supplemented by numerous creeks, including Kearsley Creek, Thread Creek and Misteguay Creek. The Flint River empties into the Shiawassee River in the Shiawassee National Wildlife Refuge near Saginaw.

The river is dammed in several locations. In Richfield Township, the dam forms the Holloway Reservoir. The C.S. Mott Dam west of Genesee forms

Mott Lake and was completed in 1972 for recreational use. Many local attractions sit along the lake, including Crossroads Village and Huckleberry Railroad, the *Genesee Belle* riverboat, Bluebell Beach and Stepping Stone Falls. The Utah Dam, completed in 1928, has been open for decades and no longer impedes water flow. The Hamilton Dam in downtown Flint was constructed in 1920. After years of neglect, the dam had deteriorated. In March 2018, demolition began as part of the Flint Riverfront Restoration Project. An inflatable Fabri Dam that was constructed in 1979 and located downstream of the Hamilton Dam was also removed as part of the restoration project. The view of the Flint River from the Harrison Bridge is very different now.

In the downtown Flint area, the river runs by many landmarks and notable locations, including Riverbank Park, the University of Michigan–Flint, Kettering University, the Durant-Dort Carriage Company Office, Factory One (the historic birthplace of General Motors), several GM factories and the huge industrial complex once known as Chevy in the Hole. This is the location of the historic Flint Sit-Down Strikes. The area has been cleaned up and transformed into a park now known as Chevy Commons.

For decades, the river was filled with industrial pollution. But thanks to the Clean Water Act and the efforts of local organizations, the river has seen vast improvements in the past decade.

Many stories have swirled through time concerning the river and its ties to the spirit world. Many paranormal sightings in Flint have occurred along the stretch of the river between Chevy in the Hole and Buick City. All around the river, many orbs have been seen dancing along the water at night. Some believe the orbs are the souls of the many people who have died in the river's waters.

From Flint's incorporation as a city through the Great Depression, the river provided a place for bathing for a number of residents. Many did not know how to swim. The murky water, the slippery rocks and the river's current claimed the lives of more than one hundred of those bathers.

There is an old legend about a man who walks along the riverbank just after dusk near the Smith Street Bridge (now North Grand Traverse Street). He seems to be looking for someone or something. People have approached him to ask if he needs help, but he never responds. He just continues searching. As they get closer to him, he simply disappears.

There are two origin stories for this searching specter. The first one is that he was a homeless man who was robbed and killed under the bridge. He continues to search for his things that were stolen. The second story is more romantic. A young couple in love had just enjoyed a nice dinner date one

February evening and decided to go ice-skating with their friend near the Smith Street Bridge. The couple skated off to be alone for a romantic kiss when they encountered a thin piece of ice, fell in and drowned. The man's body was found down the river, but the woman's body was never found. This legend evolved from a true story that happened in 1918. Some say the man continues to look for his girlfriend, to whom he was planning on proposing the night they died.

Near the Grand Trunk railroad bridge, a block west of today's North Grand Traverse Street, many people have heard the haunting sound of a baby's cry.

Every city felt the hardship of the Great Depression, and an extra mouth to feed was more than some could bear. On August 5, 1932, the watchman at Chevrolet Motors found an infant wrapped in newspaper floating in the river. When the police arrived, they recovered the body of a baby boy fastened to a piece of iron with a wire wrapped around its neck. The coroner said the baby was believed to have been in the water for ten days and was alive at birth. The baby's cause of death was strangulation.

A few days later, three people were in custody for the murder of the infant: a woman who recently gave birth and her husband, who had five older children; and a man who was a boarder at the couple's home. The husband was released shortly after questioning. The next day, the wife and the boarder were booked on murder charges. The mother claimed she was told by the man and the father of the child that the baby was born dead. When the detective went over how they found the baby, they claimed that was not their child and that they buried their baby in the same area along the river. A second baby's body was recovered, and the two were booked on murder charges for suffocating the baby to death. They were sentenced to fifteen years in prison. The murder of the first baby was never solved, and the baby now resides in an unmarked grave in Flint.

19

DOWNTOWN FLINT

There are whispered reports of paranormal activity from locations all over downtown Flint, but not much evidence can be found to back things up, not even a first-person account of the activity.

There have been whispers from former employees about strange occurrences, spooky voices and shadowy figures at several local bars, including the Torch and Churchill's, but so far it is nothing more than third-person anecdotes.

However, there are a few downtown locations that have a deeper history to dive into.

NATIONAL GUARD ARMORY

The Flint National Guard Armory stands deserted next to Avondale Cemetery.

In 2013, it was decided that the armory would close and move to Saginaw. The building is over ninety years old and needs more than $6 million in repairs.

The Flint armory is the former headquarters for the 125th Infantry Battalion. With over twenty-five thousand square feet, the four-story building was once home base for six companies of more than seven hundred soldiers.

The Flint National Guard Armory. *Courtesy of Ari Napolitano.*

After the deadly 1953 Beecher tornado, local hospitals were overflowing with the wounded and dead. The Flint armory was set up as a temporary morgue to help the hospitals make room for the injured living who needed care.

"The scene of bodies pouring into the Armory (as an intermittent light rain poured outside) was incredibly bleak and horrifying, especially for the families and friends of the victims. At least 100 people waited outside into the rainy night before they could move inside to try and identify the bodies. Captain James Berardo of the State Police warned the people that the terrible tornado had horribly battered some victims and the scene inside would be gruesome" (AbsoluteMichigan.com).

Many rumors swirl about the old armory being haunted. A 2002 *Flint Journal* story reported that some former soldiers have claimed the building is filled with ghosts. Many Guardsmen have heard voices and footsteps in empty rooms.

Could the ghosts be tied to the trauma of the building being used a morgue?

THE DURANT HOTEL

In the early twentieth century, Flint was booming. Hotels were turning people away because they were always sold out. In December 1916, the Citizen's Hotel Company was organized for the purpose of building a new hotel on Second Avenue.

Named after the founder and president of General Motors, William C. Durant, the Durant Hotel opened its doors in December 1920. The 264-room hotel took three years to build at a cost of $2.5 million.

Hundreds of Flint's wealthiest people gathered there on New Year's Eve for its grand opening celebration. The hotel offered luxury rooms and suites that were filled to capacity so often that an addition was erected a few years after it first opened. This addition included more guest rooms, a new ballroom and the eight-room Durant Suite, named in honor of its biggest investor.

The first floor not only offered ballrooms and meeting space but also had its own shopping district inside featuring a jewelry store, bank, hat store, men's store, fur shop, florist, lingerie shop, appliance store, shoe store, coffee shop and a branch of the Genesee County Savings Bank.

The two most popular areas of the hotel were the Purple Cow Restaurant on the hotel's lobby floor on the Saginaw Street side, and the Wheel Room, an Art Deco lounge.

The hotel hosted all the major conferences, events and training for the automotive industry in Flint. It was also the desired place to stay for visiting entertainers and politicians. Frank Sinatra, Doris Day and Glenn Miller were some of the entertainers who stayed at the Durant.

In 1937, the hotel became the headquarters to negotiate an end to Flint's violent Sit-Down Strike. Governor Frank Murphy used the Durant as his headquarters while he acted as courier and intermediary between GM and the UAW and helped negotiate the end of the strike on February 11, 1937.

After almost two decades of prosperity, the hotel guests were dwindling. A major remodel was undertaken. In 1939, the number of guests continued to decline; the hotel could not make its mortgage and was foreclosed on and put up for auction. Metropolitan Life Insurance purchased the hotel in 1940. A year later, it was in default again.

In 1942, the Pick Hotel Corporation took ownership of the hotel, naming it the Pick Durant Hotel. The hotel flourished under the Pick Hotel chain for the next two decades, once again becoming the main source for meeting space for the local automotive companies.

One week before a major Buick Sales Convention in 1960, the ballroom was severely damaged by a fire. Luckily, contractors were able to rebuild the room in time for the convention. A few years later, rumors started going around about offers to sell the hotel. In 1969, Pick Corporation ended the rumors by announcing its new remodeling plans. The plans included making the rooms larger, adding a parking lot and remodeling the banquet rooms.

In 1973, as the downtown area started to decline and businesses started moving to the suburbs, the hotel closed. The Genesee County Landbank acquired the building in 2005. The boarded-up building stood as a symbol of Flint's glorious past until 2009, when plans for its reopening emerged.

In 2010, the hotel, now called the Durant Housing Complex, opened with ninety-three apartment rental units, luxury office space, storefronts and a newly renovated ballroom. In 2011, the hotel was once again at full capacity.

In the 1960s, several stories emerged about the sound of footsteps echoing in the hallway of the sixth floor. People claim that the footsteps are that of Billy Durant. In the hotel's glory days of the Roaring Twenties, an eight-room suite named the Durant Suite was often used by namesake Billy Durant during many of the General Motors events that took place at the hotel.

Could Billy Durant be reliving his glory days in the afterlife?

A postcard featuring the Hotel Durant. *Author Collection.*

Sometimes, the voices of past celebrations can be heard in the ballroom. Employees have claimed that, when all is quiet, laughter, footsteps and the sound of dancing echo through the grand ballroom.

For years after the hotel closed in 1973, the neon "Motor Hotel" sign would mysteriously light up at night. The phone number continued to be listed in the phone book, leading many people to the doors of the abandoned building thinking it was open. In 1979, there were whispered reports of a female ghost sighted on the premises

In 2008, when the hotel was under renovation, a construction worker fell out of a window. A comment on the *Flint Journal*'s online article said the Durant ghost pushed him.

Many have claimed to see a young man in his twenties walking around on the sidewalk outside the Durant where the College Inn coffee shop once stood on the corner of Detroit Street (now Martin Luther King Avenue) and Second Avenue.

On the evening of October 10, 1928, Lawrence Hutchins was walking home from an evening class at General Motors Institute when he saw brothers Sammy (a bellboy at the Durant Hotel) and Melvin Raskin harassing Ann Lovakis, a waitress at the coffee shop who was trying to leave work.

During Ann's shift, Sammy had sat in the coffee shop with his brother for hours making advances on her. Repulsed by his advances, Ann tried to sneak out at the end of her shift without Sammy noticing. Outside of the coffee shop, she was met by Sammy's brother Melvin, who held her there until Sammy noticed her departure. The two men trapped her in front of the building.

Lawrence Hutchins heard the lady's cry for help and came to her rescue. While Lawrence fought Sammy, allowing Ann to escape, Sammy's brother Melvin struck Lawrence in the jaw. The brothers ran away as Lawrence staggered along Second Avenue. He collapsed in front of one of the storefronts at the Durant Hotel. Ann rushed to help her knight. Lawrence lay there twitching until his body went still. People just passed by, afraid to help. The Raskin brothers were known around the city as people not to mess with. By the time the ambulance arrived, Hutchins was dead.

Is Lawrence Hutchins still walking the street, trying to get home?

THE MASONIC TEMPLE

Officially dedicated in 1911, the Flint Masonic Temple is located in the heart of downtown. The historic building is rich in architectural detail and offers elegant rental space for weddings and other events. The building contains three floors of rental areas plus a basement dining hall. In 2004, it was listed as a historical landmark.

When you attend an event at the Flint Masonic Temple, you might sense the spooky feeling that hangs in the air, even during happy and cheerful events like weddings, parties and craft shows.

Many people who have worked in the building have seen shadowy figures and heard strange noises they can't explain. Many have heard the faint sounds of organ music from upstairs…but no one is there and the organ is not a self-playing instrument.

One spine-tingling location is the basement. Chills have a tendency to course down your spine as you venture slowly into the darkness of the basement to find one of the restrooms. The dining room is usually closed during events, so that area is dark, and you have to pass it to get to the main restrooms. You may get lucky and a hall light is on; sometimes it isn't, and you have to make your way to the restroom in a dimly lit hall.

Renovations have not been done in decades, so the building is much the same as it was when it was built. The plumbing isn't quite as old as the building, but it sure isn't up to modern standards. Every restroom I have ventured into has an aura of oddness about it.

One of the restrooms on the Blue Floor may creep you out so bad that you trek all the way to the basement to use a restroom that doesn't give you the heebie-jeebies quite as much.

The York Floor is a red space of Gothic elegance befitting a vampire wedding and considered to be the most haunted location in the building. One night, a show director was working late and turned around to find a translucent woman in white just hovering in the doorway. The filmy apparition floated from one doorway to another then just disappeared.

During the Vampire Ball one year, a séance was held on the York Floor. Ghostly shadows filled the room. A couple of people were so terrified that they vowed never to return. Perhaps that séance opened a door for spirits to come through.

The main floor of the temple houses the auditorium, which is used for large events. It contains a stage and a large floor that can be filled with tables and chairs for a sit-down event and a second-floor mezzanine area

A postcard featuring the Masonic Temple. *Author collection.*

that can be used for extra lighting and sound for stage productions or as a VIP area.

For several years, Ted Valley had an office inside the temple on the mezzanine level for his theater group, Vertigo Theatrics. Vertigo held the annual Flint Vampire Ball at the Masonic Temple during the Halloween season and did many productions and dinner-theater events.

Valley would often work late into the night planning events and building stage props for the productions. This meant that he was often all alone in the big, old building. Valley is an admitted skeptic and won't firmly say that he "believes" in ghosts, but he's had too many encounters—most of them in the Masonic Temple—that he can't explain away.

Valley kept his desk facing the open doorway of his office. He would often get the feeling that someone walked in front of the door while he was working. Sometimes, shadows would pass across the doorway, even though he knew he was alone in the building. Occasionally, it would bother him so much that he would get up and check the area just to make sure no one was walking around.

One night, Valley was prepping for a show late into the night. He was on the red floor around 3:00 a.m. On the other side of the red floor's balcony level, there is an old locker room. The lockers contain remnants of possessions from former Masons, members long dead. He was all alone in the building, focused on the upcoming show, and suddenly he heard the lockers rattling while he was working on some wiring. He had no time for the drama of ghosts. So he yelled, "Knock it off! I'm busy working here." Everything got quiet, and he went back to work. Then, "Wham, wham, wham!" It sounded like someone slammed a locker door.

He yelled again, "Listen, I told you I'm working here! The more you screw around, the longer I'll be here. Once I get done you can go back to playing your music and doing your weird little dances." The building became quiet as a tomb.

Valley went back to work on the wiring. After a while, he heard pacing… from the ceiling. The only thing above him was an attic and the roof. The pacing was quite literally on the ceiling, back and forth, back and forth. The spirit continued pacing until Valley left for the night.

Another memorable experience Valley recalled occurred while Vertigo was putting together a production of *Jacob Marley's Christmas Carol*—perhaps the story itself riled up the spirits. It was heavily focused on showing the Christmas Carol story from Marley's point of view, and the story line predominantly featured the netherworld.

Many peculiar things happened during the production of this show. One time, an actor was standing on the stage and a light bulb came unscrewed and fell on top of his head. He wasn't hurt, but it was so odd. The light bulb had to be unscrewed for it to fall; it wasn't something that could just come loose.

One evening, several members of the group were rehearsing late into the night. No one else was in the building, just the theater members, and as they finished a scene, they heard "bam, bam, bam" on the floor above them. The Masons are well known for rituals, one of which involves a wood staff hitting the floor three times.

Valley offered a little insight into why spirits would want to hang out at the temple. Becoming a Mason was extremely important to these men. Prominent members of society worked very hard to become a Mason. Once they were part of the prestigious group, they spent a lot of time in the temple—meetings, events and so on. It's no wonder that spirits would continue to linger in a place that had been so important to them in life.

Over the years, many of Flint's most prominent citizens were masons: Walter Chrysler, J. Dallas Dort, C.S. Mott and James Whiting, to name a few. But declining membership led to the seven-story, one-hundred-plus-year-old Flint Masonic Temple going up for sale in late 2017.

In March 2018, Flint's Communities First Inc. started the paperwork to purchase the building. There is no word if the sale has been completed.

As of this writing, the Temple Dining Room remains open, and the temple continues to operate as usual for event rentals, but the Flint Masonic Lodge is no longer open for membership.

625 SOUTH SAGINAW STREET

Right down the road from the Masonic Temple, along the bricks on Saginaw Street, is a downtown Flint apartment in one of the city's historic buildings. It neighbors the Capitol Theatre. The buildings are separated by Brush Alley.

Former residents of the studio apartment were plagued by eerie occurrences while they resided there. The female resident often saw shadowy shapes and black figures, wispy things that slithered just out of view. She heard eerie voices and odd noises. Friends who stayed the night would remark that they heard strange things throughout the apartment.

One night, the couple left a video recording device in the basement of the old building. There was no video that could be seen, yet you could hear the sound of the light switch being clicked on and off in the background.

Another night, the couple left a recording device in the male's office on the first floor of the apartment. This was an area where shadowy shapes were often seen. While they slept, something creepy was caught on film. The recording picked up muttering, then a noise that sounded like scraping, as if someone had pushed back the office chair, stood up and walked across the wood floor to the bathroom, closed the door, flushed the toilet, returned to the office, muttered and sat back down. Then all was quiet once again.

SECRETS BENEATH THE CITY

Many of America's older cities have service tunnels running underneath them. Flint is no exception. There are many stories about the tunnels under the old Oak Grove Sanitarium location and the old Flint Central High School campus. One tunnel has been found that leads into Central.

But there are also stories about tunnels under the bricks of downtown Flint.

In 1909, Paterson had a tunnel built under Third Street that connected two of the old auto factories, the factory on Harrison Street and the factory on Third that was behind St. Paul's Episcopal Church. The tunnel connected the two factories so that vehicles and supplies could easily be moved between the two locations.

There are rumors of other tunnels as well.

Many of the historic buildings in downtown Flint have doors and entryways to the old tunnels in their basements, but they are welded shut or bricked up.

Under the bricks lies a mystery, an unknown history.

Do ghosts wander the abandoned tunnels, keeping watch over Flint's forgotten secrets?

20

FLINT PARK AMUSEMENT PARK AND DEVIL'S LAKE

In the northwest corner of Flint, an amusement park once stood complete with bumper cars, a Tilt-A-Whirl, a rollercade and a roller coaster. The park was located off DuPont and Stewart between Dewey Woods and Flint Park Lake (Devil's Lake).

Conceived in 1919 and opened in 1921, Flint Park Amusement Park operated through 1960. The decision was made not to reopen for the 1961 season.

The park was central to Flint's entertainment for many years. The streetcar line was even extended so fun-seekers had direct transportation to the park. The park had many rides, including a wooden roller coaster called the Jack Rabbit, the Whip, Old Mill Water Ride, a Ferris wheel, Dodgem Bumper Cars and Octopus. The lake had a lagoon area for boats and swimming. There was also a dance hall, opera house, rollercade, sports and event area and a kiddie park zone. A mini-golf course was added later.

Many carnival and musical performers appeared at the park over the years, including Ella Fitzgerald. It was an extremely popular destination for Flint residents. Many older Flint residents who were alive during the park's golden years have fond memories of riding the rides, roller skating and enjoying shows.

While it seemed like a well-loved location of fun, games and entertainment, Flint Park was not without troubles. Soon after opening in 1921, a fire broke out in the concession area, causing damage to ten concession stands. In

A postcard featuring the Midway at Flint Park Amusement Park. *Courtesy of Daniel Conner.*

December 1928, twenty-year-old Joseph Studniarz fell through the ice while skating and drowned. In the 1930s, after there were a couple deaths in the park and the adjoining lake, a dark shadow began to be cast over the glitter and glitz of the park.

On May 31, 1936, thirty-eight-year-old Charles Frazier failed to heed warnings and stood up while on the roller coaster. He was riding with his thirteen-year-old niece in the last seat of the second car and stood up when it reached the top of the first hill, fifty-eight feet in the air. As the coaster car descended, he lost his balance and fell to his death.

Daredevil aerialist Manuel Valencia's "Dance of Death" pole performance sadly became an all-too-accurate description for the show when he plunged 150 feet to his death in front of a crowd of more than one thousand spectators in June 1938. He landed at the feet of his wife and partner, Verna. At first, the crowd thought it was part of the show, until she screamed. The duo had been performing together for thirty-two years. They had one more show scheduled after Flint, and then they planned to retire.

In May 1939, twenty-eight-year-old Anna Mitoraj rowed out into Flint Park Lake, tipped her boat and drowned. Her death was ruled a suicide.

Several buildings were destroyed by fire in the offseason in January 1944. Later that year, the park was sued by a man whose son was injured when a safety strap came loose and the boy fell off a ride.

A postcard featuring the dance hall at Flint Park Amusement Park. *Courtesy of Daniel Conner.*

On Monday, June 8, 1953, the deadly Beecher tornado roared through the Flint and Beecher area, resulting in 116 deaths and injuring 844. The F5 tornado was the last tornado in the United States to result in more than 100 fatalities and is ranked as the tenth-deadliest tornado in U.S. history. A 2000 National Weather Service poll voted the Flint-Beecher tornado as the worst natural disaster in the state of Michigan in the twentieth century. The destruction was catastrophic. Beecher High School was completely destroyed, and the North Flint Drive-In was heavily damaged. A movie had been playing when the tornado hit, forcing hundreds of people to flee the drive-in theater in a panic. Over three hundred homes and businesses were annihilated. The park survived the tornado, but the roller coaster was badly damaged and needed many repairs.

The park changed hands a couple of times over the years. It continued to add rides and new features, such as 1950's "World's Largest Sideshow," but the appeal seemed to wear off, and the park became less popular. The golden years of local amusement parks were over. Vandals were an ever-increasing problem as the neighborhood declined. In March 1961, it was announced that Flint Park would not reopen.

Growing up in the '80s, I had always heard stories about "Devil's Lake," a bottomless lake that sucked people straight to hell. Anyone who attempted to swim across the lake would die.

The Hippie Conservative's blog details a tale about living by the lake:

During the course of my youth I saw several kids pulled out of that lake. Each time we would huddle as close to the divers from the rescue squads as we could. We were fascinated by their stories of what it was like down there. Giant carp and catfish, stolen cars, water thick with black pete that seems to just hang in the water. Once one of them was nearly sucked in, and now they were all tied together with rope. Finally, the crowd would become quiet and they would float the body up with balloons as we all would stare, horrified. The sound of a mother crying for her child is something that is hard to forget and it always came right as they lifted the body away from The Devil. I could easily live the rest of my life without ever hearing it again.

In October 2016, the urban legend made it into a Buzzfeed article of thirteen creepy hometown stories. This item was submitted by "rizzyb2":

There's a lake in my hometown of Flint, Michigan, called Devil's Lake which is said to have no bottom. Instead it's urban legend that it's actually an outlet to hell. It's called Devil's Lake and it's located between a park and a funeral home! Nobody who has ever attempted to swim the lake has survived to see the other side. Anybody would be too scared to jump in and save them.

Blight and vacant lots dominate the streets surrounding Flint Park Lake. For decades, the park was empty and abandoned. The edges of the lake were swampy and overgrown. There was no real access for boating or fishing. The neighborhood was filled with crime. People avoided Flint Park.

In 2008, a fifty-dollar bet ended tragically when Reginald Johnson tried to prove that old urban legend wrong by swimming across the lake.

In 2014, a lake revitalization effort was launched by the Genesee County Parks in partnership with the City of Flint. As part of the cleanup effort, sheriff's departments from Lapeer and Genesee Counties, Genesee County Parks and Recreation park rangers, along with the Genesee Auto-Theft Investigation Network, teamed up and pulled eight old vehicles from the water.

To beautify the lake and improve accessibility, dead trees and brush were cleared out, a dock was built for fishing and a picnic pavilion and playground structure were built at the site.

As an adult, I discovered that my family has ties to the Flint Park Amusement Park. I learned that my parents met while roller skating at Flint Park in 1954. Later, when I inherited my grandparents' house in the '90s, I learned that it was tied to Flint Park as well. When the park closed, my grandfather purchased the office building and had it brought to his land. He used it as a starting point to build his house—the house I now live in.

I often wonder if the building from Flint Park is the source of my home's paranormal experiences. The main area of activity was my grandmother's bedroom when she lived in the house. I never remember her actually sleeping in it. Whenever I stayed with her, she would sleep in the living room. She seemed to avoid that room. The door was always shut, and no one ever went in there.

When I first moved into the house, that room became the nursery, because it was the closest bedroom to the master suite. First, it was my oldest child's room. I never knew he had any issues with it. Now that he's an adult, he has told me about his experiences in that room, how he would listen to footsteps in the night, lying awake terrified until he finally fell asleep exhausted, hiding under the blankets. I swear he grew up to have fear-induced narcolepsy, because now he tends to fall asleep during horror movies.

When my daughter was born, it became her room. Had I known my son's problems with the room, I might not have put my baby girl in there. She never slept well in that room. She constantly fussed and cried and wanted out of her crib, though sometimes the fussing wasn't her. I would hear strange noises and crying through the baby monitor, only to walk in and find her sound asleep. One night when she was a toddler, my husband heard a strange noise after putting her to bed. He walked in the room and found all the drawers in the dresser open, yet our daughter was in her bed sound asleep. There was no way she could have opened all the drawers then crawled back in bed before he opened her door. Plus, she was still so small she couldn't even reach the top drawer.

Throughout the years, she would wake up every night and want out of that room. Once she was big enough to have a toddler bed, she would leave her room and crawl in bed with me or go to her big brother and crawl in bed with him. Once we moved her to another room, she slept in her own bed just fine.

My youngest—he absolutely refused to have anything to do with that room. Ever. That room has a tendency to creep most of the family out. Whenever one of us is home alone, the door gets closed.

Now that room is my husband's office and man cave. More than once, I've been home alone and the television in there turned on all by itself. The house would be completely quiet, then all of a sudden…voices. Terror gripped me until I realized it was coming from a TV. Then another jolt of fear ran through me as I realized it was coming from *that room* and that there was no explanation for the TV coming on by itself. The door was closed, there were no cats in the room, which meant no paws to step on the remote and accidentally turn it on (which they have done in the living room a few times).

My husband has had several unexplained encounters in there. Many times, he has seen a dark figure walk through the room and stand by the window as if looking out, searching. One night, he had an entire conversation with a female teenager that no one else could see. It could have been the Valium he was on. But the story spooked me, because she was around the same age as our daughter, and having a female "teen" ghost fit with the fact that several times I had heard a female sneeze and a young woman's voice, even though I was alone in the house.

My husband and oldest son have spotted a middle-aged woman, her hair in a bun, dressed in 1950s-style business attire walk through the living room and vanish. This tends to happen around 7:00 a.m. on Saturday mornings. She does not seem to be a sentient spirit. I have often wondered if she worked at Flint Park and is just a residual haunting, a memory imprint playing on a loop.

My husband and other males have also seen another, older woman in the house from time to time. A couple of my daughter's friends have asked her "Who's the old woman on the couch?" or "Who's that old lady in the kitchen?" No one else could see an old woman.

One night, my husband walked out of his room and turned white as a ghost himself. He looked toward the kitchen and said, "There's an old woman standing in the doorway…but I know she's not really there." I was spooked the entire night, constantly looking over my shoulder to see if I could catch a glimpse of her. Now he'll just randomly say, "The old woman is standing by the television" or "The old woman is on the couch."

My husband has described the appearance of the manifestation to me, but the description doesn't seem to fit my grandmother, even though two psychics and a couple of "sensitives" have said they feel her presence in the home protecting me.

There have been many other odd occurrences in the house, like the basement door that opens by itself, numerous things that simply disappear and the music that you can hear off in the distance but can never quite make out the words or the tune. You can check every room in the house, but you will never find the source.

We've gotten used to the haunts and usually joke about them.

But a few incidents have shaken me up pretty bad. And they occurred in my bedroom, the one room in the house that had always been a safe haven for me, the room free of creepiness. Until one night I was roused from sleep by the creaking of my floorboards.

All around my bedroom, the old floors creak when you walk on them. Even I have a hard time avoiding the creaky spots because they surround my bed.

One night, I woke up to the sound of someone pacing back and forth at the end of my bed. I could tell the location of the movement of whatever it was by the distinct creaks the boards make. I was paralyzed with fear. I knew no one could have been in my room. The door never opened. I used to immediately wake up when my door opened, thanks to the loud scraping sound it made from sticking in the door frame. (My husband has since replaced the door, so, thankfully, it no longer does that.)

I laid there listening to the pacing movement. I tried to listen for anything else—breathing, a voice…but there was nothing. Finally, I took a deep breath, gathered my courage and sat up with my eyes wide open, ready to confront the pacing spirit. The sound abruptly stopped, and of course, nothing was there.

A few nights later, I awoke to a strange sound. It was a weird rattling, shaking noise. Nonstop. It just kept shaking. I couldn't take it. I got up, turned on my light and began to search the room for the annoying noise. I found the sound on my desk. It was my bobblehead turtle, Bob. His head was bobbling as though an invisible hand was shaking him at warp speed. Yet the rest of him was not moving. Nothing else was moving. Nothing in the room was rattling, vibrating or shaking. Just his head, moving extremely fast.

I stood there in shock and just stared at him. Finally, I grabbed his head and stopped it from moving. I picked him up and looked closely at him. I shook him really fast. No matter what I did, I could not make his head repeat its previous movement. It seemed humanly impossible to replicate that movement.

I took Bob out of the room. He was banished. Now I tend to find him in odd places when I clean, like under my desk, in my closet, under my bed. I have no idea where he is at this moment. Frankly, I don't care, as long as his head never moves like that again.

I don't know what or who was trying to get my attention that week, nor do I know why. I saged and salted my room. For a long time, nothing else happened.

Then one night, I was once again awoken by creaking floorboards. But this time, something felt really off. For the first time, I was really terrified in my home. This entity was not one of my normal spirits. Anger and menace, something negative had permeated my room.

I was going to turn my head and look, but something stopped me. It felt like a hand on my forehead. It held me in place and covered my eyes, as if telling me, "No, don't look."

So I didn't. I lay there, filled with terror, barely able to breathe until the pressure on my head was gone and the creaking of the floorboards stopped. When the sinister feeling dissipated, the room became calm and still. I opened my eyes and sat up. Nothing was there.

After that, a thorough metaphysical cleansing was performed on my room. I added protection crystals and symbols. Later, a psychic came in and cleansed our entire house. Some strange things still occur, but nothing sinister. We're back to the normal benign spirits of our odd haunted house.

CONCLUSION

The dark tapestry that is the city of Flint has been woven with betrayal, poverty, death, murder, scandal, sickness and tragedy, yet gold and silver threads of hope and perseverance continue to make this small city glitter and shine against all odds.

You would think that the high crime rates would make it hard to rebuild the city of Flint. Who wants to live in or invest in an area filled with crime? Yet somehow, downtown Flint continues to rebuild. It may have been down for a couple decades, but it seems to be coming back, stronger than ever, because people are willing to invest in it and bring it back to life.

The historic Capitol Theatre, which sat empty for decades, recently reopened after a multimillion-dollar renovation. The Riverfront Restoration Project is underway. The project includes the removal of the Hamilton Dam, the greening of Riverbank Park and the former Chevy in the Hole site and the construction of a walking bridge to connect the statewide Iron Belle Trail. Many of downtown Flint's buildings that have sat empty for years have recently been renovated or are in the process of being renovated. The Marketplace—a housing complex planned for the site of the old YWCA between Stevens and Wallenberg Streets—is in the works. The Marketplace development will include ground-level commercial space and ninety-two apartments, with forty-eight of the units designed to be affordable downtown housing.

Demolition of blighted buildings began in November 2018 at 126 and 116 Kearsley Street to allow the construction of a Hilton Hotel. The $37.9

million Hilton project includes renovation of the eleven-story former Genesee Bank building at 352 South Saginaw Street into a new 101-room hotel. The hotel will feature a banquet center and a restaurant on the second floor and a rooftop deck. The Genesee County State Savings Bank building has sat empty for a very long time.

The Ferris wheel resides in the former Ferris Bros. Furs Building, which closed in 1920. The building provides space for over thirty-nine businesses. Mott Community College's new Culinary Institute will reside in the long-vacant Woolworth Building, and the old Perry Drug Store is the new site of the Buckham Gallery, along with ELGA Credit Union and KeLan Foard the Brand. The downtown Flint business area continues to grow.

But once you get a block or two away from the bricks, the ghost towns emerge. Residential neighborhoods are still full of blight and decay, with very few living residents left. The empty spaces are haunted by the ghosts of Flint's past, of what once was.

But even on the outskirts of the downtown area, there is progress. Communities First Inc. broke ground on the former Coolidge Elementary School property in September 2018. The former school is being transformed into Coolidge Park Apartments, which will include fifty-four apartments, 9,600 square feet of commercial space and more than 9,000 square feet of community space.

Clark Commons is a $16.9 million development on Flint's north side, off Saginaw Street. This project is creating a six-block neighborhood development with eleven buildings. It will include sixty-two mixed-income units. Located at the northwest point of the Cultural Center Campus at the corner of Robert T. Longway Boulevard and Chavez Drive, the Flint Cultural Center Academy will be a free public school with a focus on arts education. It is expected to open in the fall of 2019 with 300 students in kindergarten through fifth grade. By 2022, they hope to accommodate 650 kindergarten through eighth-grade students.

After many years of economic devastation and depression, forward-thinking businesspeople are once again investing in Flint. Perhaps if things continue to go well and the city continues to rebuild, the new energy will put the old ghosts to rest and bring about another era of innovation and prosperity.

BIBLIOGRAPHY

Books

Bald, F.C. *Detroit's First American Decade, 1796 to 1805*. Ann Arbor: University of Michigan Press, 1948.

Crawford, Kim. *The Daring Trader: Jacob Smith in the Michigan Territory, 1802–1825*. East Lansing: Michigan State University Press, 2012.

Ellis, Franklin. *The History of Genesee County, Michigan*. Philadelphia: Everts & Abbott, 1879.

Flinn, Gary. *Hidden History of Flint*. Charleston, SC: The History Press, 2010.

———. *Remembering Flint, Michigan: Stories from the Vehicle City*. Charleston, SC: The History Press, 2010.

Headlight Flashes Along the Grand Trunk Railway System; Flint, Michigan. Chicago: Chicago Railroad Publishing, 1896.

Tedsen, Kathleen, and Beverly Rydel. *Haunted Travels of Michigan Volume II*. Holt, MI: Thunder Bay Press, 2010.

———. *Stepping into Darkness*. Holt, MI: Thunder Bay Press, 2017.

Wood, Edwin O. *History of Genesee County, Michigan, Her People, Industries, and Institutions*. Indianapolis, IN: Federal Publishing, 1916.

Young, Gordon. *Tear Down: Memoir of a Vanishing City*. Los Angeles: University of California Press, 2013.

Magazine and Newspaper Articles

Acosta. Roberto. "Have $500,000? You Could Buy Flint's Historic Masonic Temple." Mlive.com, November 30, 2017. https://www.mlive.com.

———. "A Look at the Whaley Historic House Museum in Flint through the Years." Mlive.com, November 30, 2015. https://www.mlive.com.

———. "3 Businesses Moving into Former Perry Drugs Building in Downtown Flint." Mlive.com, January 8, 2019. https://www.mlive.com.

Adams, Dominic. "Flint Schools Sitting on Two Dozen Closed Buildings in the City." Mlive.com, October 2, 2015. https://www.mlive.com.

———. "Flint Violent Crime Rate Up 23 Percent, New FBI Stats Show." Mlive.com, September 24, 2018. https://www.mlive.com.

Atkinson, Scott. "Back to the Bricks: Flint's Glenwood Cemetery Shares Tales of Those Who Revolutionized the World." Mlive.com. July 16, 2013. https://www.mlive.com.

———. "Lost Orphans: How One Woman Found the Forgotten Students of Michigan School for the Deaf." Mlive.com, September 19, 2014. https://www.mlive.com.

Berg, Jackie. "Business Growth in Flint's Downtown District Shows Promising Signs." *Hub Flint*, June 4, 2018.

Campbell, Bob. "Flash Floods Sock It to Flint." *Detroit Free Press*, September 7, 1985.

Dennison, Cheryl. "Spooktacular Stuff Holly Hotel & the Oak Grove Sanitarium." *My City Magazine*, October 3, 2016. http://www.mycitymag.com.

Detroit Free Press. "Dies in Doctor's Arms." September 6, 1908.

———. "Heiress Held in Sanitarium Wins Freedom." September 25, 1915.

———. "New Amusement Devices Offer Thrill." June 19, 1927.

———. "Scouts, Army Hunt Woman." September 30, 1979.

———. "Skater Drowned at Flint Park." December 23, 1928.

———. "Son of Wealthy Widow Hunted by Police After She Is Beaten to Death." May 28, 1933.

———. "A Verdict of Suicide." November 10, 1897.

Dolezal, Susan. "Flood Devastates House, Hopes." *Detroit Free Press*, September 16, 1985.

Dresden, Eric. "Flint Sit-Down Strike Gave Blue Collar Workers 'Respect in the Workplace,' UAW Official Says on 78th Anniversary." Mlive.com, December 30, 2014. https://www.mlive.com.

Dudar, Hasan. "Report: Detroit, Flint, Saginaw Among 10 Most Dangerous U.S. Cities." *Detroit Free Press*, May 8, 2018.

Eagle, Julie. "$30 Million Lawsuit Is Latest Chapter in Saga of Estate." *South Florida Sun Sentinel*, April 17, 1985.

Flanigan, Brian. "Flint Mom's Body Is Found, Son Is Held." *Detroit Free Press*, April 7, 1980.

Flinn, Gary. "Haunted Places in Downtown Flint." *Your Magazine*, October 2008.

Fonger, Ron. "50 Years Later: Ghosts of Corruption Still Linger Along Old Path of Failed Flint Water Pipeline." Mlive.com, November 12, 2012. https://www.mlive.com.

Goodin-Smith, Oona. "100-Room Hilton Hotel, Restaurant Proposed for Downtown Flint." Mlive.com, September 20, 2017. https://www.mlive.com.

Hinterman, Peter. "Flint through the Decades: Part One Industry Awakens (1900–1919)." *My City Magazine*, January 3, 2019.

Johnston, Jeff. "Eerie Tales Swirl Around Stately Flint Home—And It's for Sale." Mlive.com, October 27, 2007. https://www.mlive.com.

Ketchumm III, William. "Pieces of Flint's History Lost in Fire at Whaley Historic House Museum." Mlive.com, November 30, 2015. https://www.mlive.com.

Lawlor, Joe. "Bones Found at Stone Street Development Could Be Remains of Sauk Indians Killed in Battle Considered by Some 'Myth.'" Mlive.com, December 5, 2008. http://www.mlive.com.

LeDuff, Charlie. "Inside a Broken Police Department in Flint, Michigan." *New Yorker*, February 25, 2018.

Longley, Kristin. "Ancestral Remains Recovered from American Indian Burial Ground in Flint." Mlive.com, December 4, 2009. http://www.mlive.com.

———. "Saginaw Chippewa Tribe Reburies Remains of 67 Ancestors in Flint." Mlive.com, November 13, 2010. http://www.mlive.com.

May, Jake. "19th Century Victorian Style Highlighted in Whaley House Restoration." Mlive.com, April 4, 2018. https://www.mlive.com.

McCormick, Kenneth F. "Balfe MacDonald Set Free After 6 Years in Prison Cell." *Detroit Free Press*, February 1, 1940.

McCormick, Ken, and James Sullivan. "Swollen River Threatens Flint in Wake of Tornado." *Detroit Free Press*, May 14, 1936.

McGhan, Meredith. "Oak Grove Hospital: Combining Nature and Amusement to Heal." *On the Town Magazine*, September 27, 2017. https://beonthetown.com.

Mickel, Bryn. "Worker Falls from Durant Hotel: Injury at Historic City Hotel Prompts New Labor Outcry." Mlive.com, September 8, 2008. https://www.mlive.com.

Mlive.com. "Flint Tries to Hire Police with Pay Less than Janitors, Manicurists, and Bellhops." September 13, 2017. https://www.mlive.com.

Mostafavi, Beata. "Mott Community College Returns Native American Remains Unknowingly Stored in Artifacts Room." Mlive.com, January 12, 2009. http://www.mlive.com.

Nagl, Kurt. "Dozens of Headstones Vandalized, Flint History Damaged." Mlive.com, May 7, 2015. https://www.mlive.com.

Nixon, Alex. "Human Remains Found at Construction Site Are Indians, Police Say." *Kalamazoo Gazette*, January 30, 2008.

Ridley, Gary. "Empty School Buildings in Flint Now Magnets for Crime and Arson." Mlive.com, October 1, 2015. https://www.mlive.com.

Roberts, Larry. "General Motors Closes Buick City Complex in Flint, Michigan." World Socialist Web Site, July 2, 1999. https://www.wsws.org.

Rosbury, Allison. "Swept Away: The Flood of 1947." *My City Magazine*, September 1, 2015. http://www.mycitymag.com.

Ruble, Kayla. "The Unraveling of Flint: How 'Vehicle City' Stalled Long Before the Water Crisis." Vice News, January 26, 2016. https://news.vice.com.

Schuch, Sarah. "Kettering University Students Help Create Co-work Space, Innovation Hub in Downtown Flint." Hub Flint. January 24, 2018.

Sinnott, Jessica Pressley. "Glenwood Cemetery: A Place of Peace." *My City Magazine*, October 1, 2013.

———. "A Jacob of All Trades." *My City Magazine*, March 2, 2015.

Stebbins, Samuel, and Evan Comen. "50 Worst Cities to Live In. These Are the Worst Cities to Live in Based on Quality of Life." *USAToday*, June 13, 2018.

St. Louis Post-Dispatch. "Helen Joy Morgan Held on Murder Charges." April 26, 1931.

Thompson, Sharisse. "Families Say Flint's Avondale Cemetery Is Still Being Vandalized." NBC25 News. June 2, 2016. https://nbc25news.com.

Witkos, Matthew. "Tentative Sale of Flint's Masonic Temple Leaves Temple Dining Room Eatery in Limbo." ABC 12, March 28, 2018. https://www.abc12.com.

Yapalater, Lauren. "13 Creepy Hometown Stories that Will Scare the Shit Out of You." Buzzfeed, October 13, 2016. https://www.buzzfeed.com.

Young, Gordon. "Faded Glory: Polishing Flint's Jewels" *New York Times*. August 19, 2009. https://www.nytimes.com.

Young, Molly. "Downtown Flint River Landscape to Change as Part of $36.8M Project." MLive.com, May 10, 2017. https://www.mlive.com/news/flint/index.ssf/2017/05/downtown_flint_river_landscape.html.

From the Web

ABC12.com. "Homeless Man Found Dead Near Vacant Flint Warehouse." January 7, 2019. https://www.abc12.com.

Alarms.org. "Top 100 Most Dangerous Cities in America." https://www.alarms.org.

CNN. "Flint Water Crisis Fast Facts." Last updated December 6, 2018. https://www.cnn.com/2016/03/04/us/flint-water-crisis-fast-facts/index.html.

Greenwood Historical Cemetery. "Welcome to Glenwood Cemetery." https://glenwoodhistoricalcemetery.org.

Gribben, Mark. "Losing It All." The Malefactor's Register. http://malefactorsregister.com/wp/a-love-not-meant-to-last.

The Hippie Conservative. "The Devil in the Lake." August 12, 2007. http://thehippieconservative.blogspot.com.

History.com. "March 5, 1929 David Buick Dies." November 13, 2009. https://www.history.com/this-day-in-history/david-buick-dies.

Major-Smolinski.com. "Young but Deadly—Balfe MacDonald." https://major-smolinski.com.

MLive.com. "A Brief History of General Motors Corp." September 14, 2008. https://www.mlive.com/business/index.ssf/2008/09/a_brief_history_of_general_mot.html.

Michigan.gov. "Historical Marker—L1396C—Jacob Smith / Fred A. Aldrich (Marker ID#:L1396C)." http://www.michigandnr.com/publications/pdfs/ArcGISOnline/StoryMaps/mhc_historical_markers/pdfs/MHC251989005.pdf.

Motor City Ghost Hunters. "Robert Whaley House, Flint, MI June 28th, 2014." July 28, 2014. http://motorcityghosthunters.com.

Native-Languages.org. "Native American Legends: Flint (Tawiscara, Warty)." http://www.native-languages.org/morelegends/flint.htm.

The Necro Tourist. "Necro Tour Guides for Haunted Cemeteries in Michigan." http://www.thefuneralsource.org/necrotourist/guides/michigan/haunted.html.

Teelander, Alan. "Flint Michigan History and Early North American Indians" Images of Michigan. August 6, 2012. https://www.imagesofmichigan. com/flint-michigan-history-and-early-north-american-indians.

Whaley House. "Whaley House History." http://www.whaleyhouse.com/ history.html.

Williams College Computer Science. "Iroquois Creation Myth." http:// www.cs.williams.edu/~lindsey/myths/myths_12.html.

ABOUT THE AUTHORS

Flint native Roxanne Rhoads is an author, book publicist and lover of all things spooky. She is the owner of Bewitching Book Tours, a virtual book tour and social media marketing company, and she operates *A Bewitching Guide to All Things Halloween*, a blog dedicated to Halloween How Tos, costumes, pumpkins, party planning and everything Halloween-related. When not reading, writing or promoting, Roxanne loves to craft, plan Halloween adventures and search for unique vintage finds.

Joe Schipani is an integral part of Flint's art community, with ties to local artists, galleries, bookstores and the Flint Cultural Center. He is the executive director of the Flint Public Art Project and the FFAR project assistant at the Community Foundation of Greater Flint. He has a weekly column on the blog *A Bewitching Guide to All Things Halloween*, titled "Freaky Flint History," showcasing true crime and weird but true tales of Flint deaths.

Visit us at
www.historypress.com